Family Finance

Ann Douglas

PRENTICE HALL CANADA

Canadian Cataloguing in Publication Data

Douglas, Ann, 1963–
         Family finance: the essential guide for Canadian parents

Includes index.
ISBN 0-13-022257-7

1. Finance, Personal. 2. Parents — Finance, Personal. I. Title

HG179.D675 1999   332.024'0431   C99-931808-X

Prentice-Hall Canada Inc.
Scarborough, Ontario

Prentice-Hall, Inc., Upper Saddle River, New Jersey
Prentice-Hall International (UK) Limited, London
Prentice-Hall of Australia, Pty. Limited, Sydney
Prentice-Hall Hispanoamericana, S.A., Mexico City
Prentice-Hall of India Private Limited, New Delhi
Prentice-Hall of Japan, Inc., Tokyo
Simon & Schuster Southeast Asia Private Limited, Singapore
Editora Prentice-Hall do Brasil, Ltda., Rio de Janeiro

ISBN 0-13-022257-7

Editorial Director, Trade Group: Andrea Crozier
Acquisitions Editor: Nicole de Montbrun
Copy Editor: Lisa Berland
Production Editor: Jodi Lewchuk
Art Direction: Mary Opper
Cover Design: Gary Beelik
Cover Illustration: Sandy Nichols
Interior Design: Sarah Battersby
Production Coordinator: Barbara Ollerenshaw
Page Layout: Christine Velakis

1 2 3 4 5 B-G/TPI 03 02 01 00 99
Printed and bound in Canada.

Visit the Prentice Hall Canada Web site! Send us your comments, browse our catalogues, and
more. **www.phcanada.com**.

DEDICATION

To Julie, Scott, Erik, and Ian, my four little tax deductions

CONTENTS

Family Finance

Acknowledgments

I would like to take this opportunity to thank the members of the Family Finance book panel, who shared intimate details of their families' financial affairs with me over the past three months: Leigh Abthorpe, Heidi Anderson, Ken Barker, Nicole Barker, Angel Blake, Laurie Caloren, Rose Carré, Anne Cavicchi, Diane Dronyk, Stephanie Estabrook, Paul Forget, Laura Gazley, LaRee Goddu, Lori Harasem-Mitchell, Anne Hoover, Amber Jackson, Fiona Lozinski, Louise Chatterton Luchuk, Jackie McEachern, Heather McKinnon, Cindy Mount, Kathie O'Gorman, Kristin Reynolds, Karen Rolfe, David Smith, Sharon Smythe, Mary Spicer, Laura Ann Tripp, Melinda Tuck, Pilaar Yule, Susan Yusishen, as well as those panel members who chose to share their experience anonymously.

I would also like to sincerely thank Larry Boldt, Jason Quick, and Rick Foeller, C.A., for their insightful comments on the manuscript; my lawyer, Ross Whittington, for allowing me to reproduce a modified version of the will he wrote for me in this book; Tracy Keleher of Canadian Parents Online, for sending so many book panel members my way; Robert Harris, Dean Hannaford, and Joan Whitman, my former editors at Prentice Hall, for coming up with the concept for the book and thinking of me when it was time to start shopping around for an author; Andrea Crozier, Nicole de Montbrun, Jodi Lewchuk, and Lisa Berland, the new team of editors at Prentice Hall, for their unwavering enthusiasm for the book; Sarah Battersby for working her design magic and making the book look so terrific; and my long-suffering husband, Neil, for continuing to put up with my book habit.

Introduction: Why a book about family finance?

While the bookstore shelves are overflowing with books on personal finance, what's been missing up until now is a book that's written specifically for the people who need it most: parents with young children. Some skeptics might argue that there's no need for a financial planning book for parents. After all, why should the rules of the financial planning game change just because you've got a baby drooling on your shoulder?

A whole new ball game

Like it or not, the rules of the game do change significantly the moment you become a parent. That eight-pound bundle of joy changes everything about your life, including your financial situation.

You already know how much having a baby has changed your eating and sleeping patterns. (Remember: there was a time in the not-so-distant past when you could sleep in as late as you wanted on weekends; when your idea of eating out meant sitting down in a restaurant rather than hitting the local fast food restaurant drive!) What you might not have stopped to consider, however, is just how much becoming a parent has changed your financial habits as well.

If you're like most new parents, you have probably experienced a fair bit of turbulence on the financial front since your baby first arrived on the scene:

- Your household income may have been through a roller coaster ride since junior made his grand entrance. You might have seen your household income shrink significantly while you or your partner were on maternity leave, or disappear altogether if you decided to take an extended, unpaid leave or quit your job to stay at home with your baby.
- You may have seen your personal debt levels skyrocket if your income dropped but you failed to adjust your spending habits. (I know: you don't have to be a rocket scientist to figure out that you need to cut back on your expenditures when your income takes a hit, but a surprising number of couples fall into this trap after baby arrives. I personally think this problem arises because the majority of new parents are too

sleep-deprived to worry about financial matters. After all, given the choice between sitting down and setting a budget or flopping out on the couch while your colicky baby snatches a catnap in the baby swing, most parents will hit the couch in a second.)

- Instead of spending your paycheques on clothes and entertainment as you no doubt did in your prebaby days, these days you're more likely to spend your hard-earned cash on stuff for the baby: diapers, clothes, toys, baby equipment, and so on. In fact, I'd be prepared to hazard a guess that your baby is the best-dressed member of the family. (Kind of makes you wonder why she's willing to spend so much time slumming with adults who spend their nonworking hours living in sweatshirts that are covered in every conceivable baby-related stain, now doesn't it!)

- You may find it increasingly hard to relate to the financial planning advertisements you see on TV. After all, how can you dutifully max out your RRSP or RESP contributions if you're scrambling to find enough cash to buy a new car seat for your toddler? Similarly, all the hype about mutual funds may leave you scratching your head and wondering if you're doing something wrong: Do other families with young children actually have the money to invest in anything other than diapers?

- You may have recently become a homeowner for the very first time, urged to take the plunge by that classic prebaby nesting urge that makes real estate agents rub their hands in glee. If you've been renting up until now, you could find yourself in for a bit of a rough ride financially if you drained your chequing account to pay for the lawyer's fees, the land transfer tax, and so on and find yourself hit with one of the unpleasant surprises of home ownership. If, for example, the furnace packs it in on the coldest night of the year or a pipe bursts and sends water pouring through your kitchen ceiling, there's no landlord to call to make the problem go away. Like it or not, the buck stops with you and your chequebook.

- You may find yourself thinking about life insurance, wills, powers of attorney, and other heavy-duty financial issues for the very first time. Now that you're responsible for a child, you may feel a pressing need to create a safety net for your growing family by putting your affairs in order—something that may take you by surprise if you've always taken a fly-by-the-seat-of-your-pants approach to life.

Information overload

It's not difficult to see why many parents with young children find themselves feeling overwhelmed by the amount of financial information they need to master to make the best possible choices for their families. There are so many complex—and conflicting—issues to consider before you can map out a financial game plan for your family that it's easier to ignore the whole subject entirely.

Then there's the time crunch that most families with young children face. Who has the time or the inclination to pour through financial planning books or to make sense of those mind-numbingly boring annual reports that the mutual fund companies love to send out?

That's why this book has been organized in bite-sized chunks—so that you can read it as your schedule and to-do list allow. You can either read the book from front to back or you can hop from chapter to chapter, zeroing in on the topics that are of greatest interest to you at a particular time. Either way, you'll find that the book is packed with practical, no-nonsense tips on dealing with the key financial challenges faced by couples with young children, including

- keeping your debt level under control when there are a million-and-one demands on your paycheque
- avoiding the money-related conflicts that cause problems for so many couples
- deciding whether it makes financial sense for you (or your partner) to continue working after you start your family
- identifying your financial goals and coming up with a game plan that will allow you to achieve them
- determining whether you should focus your efforts on paying down your mortgage, starting a registered educational savings plan for your child, or contributing to an RRSP
- finding ways to save money on as many items in your family's budget as possible—from food to clothing to utilities to automotive expenses to bank charges
- starting a nest egg so that you'll have funds available in the event that life tosses an unexpected curve ball your way
- making sure that you're taking advantage of the tax breaks that are available to families with young children and
- raising money-smart kids

What you won't find in this book

What you won't find in this book is preachy advice from a so-called expert who makes you feel like some kind of financial incompetent because you didn't start contributing to your RRSP when you landed your first paper route—or who shakes her head in disgust when she learns that you waste money on donut shop coffee even though there's a perfectly good coffeemaker wasting away on your kitchen counter. I'm no financial planning guru, just a mom of four who's earned a Ph.D. in money management through the School of Hard Knocks.

You won't benefit from just my experience as you read this book, of course. You'll also hear first-hand accounts of the financial challenges faced by other families. More than 50 parents agreed to share the most intimate details of their financial lives with me as I was researching this book—the good, the bad, and the ugly. They told me about the mistakes they made that took them to the brink of bankruptcy and how they managed to get themselves back on solid financial ground; and they offered practical tips on saving money on mortgages, car loans, groceries, and more. Because of their input, *Family Finance* is packed with gems of wisdom that you won't find in any other financial planning book: first-hand advice from real parents who've been there, done that—and lived to tell!

I hope you enjoy the book.

Ann Douglas

One

That Was Then, This Is Now

"We went from two incomes supporting two people to one income supporting three people!"
– Leigh, 31, mother of two.

It's a topic that prenatal classes don't cover and financial planning books generally choose to ignore: just how dramatically your financial priorities can change once you decide to take the plunge and become a parent.

It's not difficult to see why your priorities tend to evolve once you start having children. For the first time in your life, there's more to consider than how much money you have to spend on eating out or sprucing up your wardrobe. Suddenly you have to start thinking about heavy-duty financial issues like life insurance, RESPs, and mortgages.

Cindy, 40, who gave birth to twins five years ago, found that the financial changes brought on by parenthood were huge: "We went from buying grownup toys to children's toys: from planning exotic vacations to planning for family fun time and from buying leather pants to buying plastic pants! Did starting our family require a big financial adjustment on our part? In a major way!"

Show Me the Money!

Start setting aside some money each week from the moment you find out that you're pregnant. If you get in the saving habit early in your pregnancy, you should have a nice nest egg to rely on when it's time to start shopping for baby. Pregnancy is also a great time to focus on paying off any personal debt you've acquired over the years. Who knows? If you're lucky, you might even manage to get rid of your own student loan before you have to start saving for junior's education!

The financial heebie-jeebies

Some couples find that they start rethinking their financial habits the moment the pregnancy test comes back positive.

"Overnight, our priority became the children," recalls Diane, a 29-year-old mother of two. "All our money was spent on things for the baby and what the baby might need in the future."

"Before becoming pregnant, I was quite relaxed about money and only had myself to worry about," adds Stephanie, a 26-year-old mother of one. "Staring a family made me want to have an emergency fund—to start putting money away as savings, something I had never done before."

"Having a child changed how I thought about financial matters," notes Christine, 24. "Before that, I was in university, having fun and living life to its fullest, but with the birth of my daughter, I realized that I had to start saving money, spending less on myself and spending everything on her. Mutual funds, education plans, life insurance—these became my priorities."

Money Talk

"I always worked a lot and we always had extra money to spend. Money worries have been the most stressful thing about parenting so far!"
- Lori, 27, mother of one.

Your financial habits are likely to undergo a more dramatic transformation if you and your partner decide to go from two incomes to one after your children arrive.

Kate and David, 40-year-old parents of two young children, made debt reduction a priority once they knew that there was a baby on the way: "We really focussed on paying off my husband's student loan prior to my leaving my employment in order to eliminate the burden of that debt," Kate recalls.

For Melinda, a 33-year-old mother of three, the emphasis was on reducing household expenses: "After our first child was born, we sold my car. We had to relearn our spending habits and figure out how to cut corners everywhere."

Of course, not everyone has the luxury of getting their financial house in order prior to starting a family. If, as is the case with many couples, your pregnancy is unplanned, the financial fallout can be considerable. "My family was started by accident," says Heidi, a 23-year-old single parent. "It was a totally major adjustment for me. I was living with my mother, making $12 an hour, and spending every cent I earned on whatever. I didn't have a car or any real bills. I had no concept of bills, rent, daycare fees, groceries, and so on. I did not budget for anything. It was only after my son was a year old that I finally managed to be self-reliant and move out of my mother's house."

On the other hand, not every parent-to-be finds it necessary to undergo a total financial transformation the moment the pregnancy test comes back positive. Many are surprised by how *little* their financial situation changes when they start their families. "I have always lived on a budget, saved for rainy days, and looked to the future," explains Krista, a 32-year-old mother of one. "So when Ryan was born, I didn't find it hard to make the budget continue to work. Ryan's needs came first and I made sure he didn't go without. We would just go without somewhere else. This wasn't hard for us because we lived like this even before he was born."

More often than not, however, there are some lifestyle changes involved—a fact that leaves parents like 24-year-old Christine feeling grateful that expectant parents have nine months to get their financial act together: "Pregnancy gives you time to prepare for the changes that having a baby bring, even financial ones. When you look at diapers, formula, food, clothes, you realize how quickly money is spent. Having a baby was a major financial adjustment, but not one that happened overnight. My situation changed rather gradually, along with my belly."

the Bottom line

Paul and Cyndie, both 34, decided to postpone starting their family until they were in their late 20s. That gave them the opportunity to establish their careers and sow their financial wild oats before they became parents. Paul explains: "One of the main reasons that held me back from having kids earlier in life was my worry that it would have a major impact on our finances.... However, the very fact that we were ready for a family reshaped our financial priorities. We were ready to settle down. We had done some travelling and led a pretty full social life. Once Nicolas came along, outings, events, and trips were no longer important."

What it really costs to have children

The latest statistics about the cost of raising children are enough to scare prospective parents into refilling that birth control pill prescription again. According to the Centre for International Statistics at the Canadian Council on Social Development, in 1998, the cost of raising a boy to age 18 was $159,927 and the cost of raising a girl to age 18 was $158,826 (see Table 1.1).

Table 1.1: The cost of raising children
Cost of raising a boy to age 18

Age	Food	Clothing	Health care	Personal care	Recreation, reading, gifts, school needs	Transportation	Child care	Shelter, furnishings, household operation	Total
Infant	1,274	1,679	206	0	0	0	4,363	1,928	9,450
1	997	459	206	87	394	0	5,963	2,006	10,113
2	1,080	467	206	87	394	0	4,988	1,975	9,197
3	1,080	467	277	87	394	0	4,988	1,943	9,235
4	1,479	475	277	87	394	0	4,988	1,943	9,641
5	1,479	475	277	87	486	44	4,988	1,943	9,778
6	1,479	594	277	87	567	44	3,626	1,943	8,617
7	1,605	594	277	83	794	44	3,626	1,943	8,966
8	1,605	594	277	83	794	44	3,626	1,943	8,966
9	1,605	632	277	83	794	44	3,626	1,943	9,003
10	1,806	632	277	83	794	44	3,626	1,943	9,205
11	1,806	632	277	83	794	44	3,626	1,943	9,205
12	1,806	1,105	291	152	811	370	0	1,943	6,479
13	1,969	1,105	291	152	811	370	0	1,943	6,641
14	1,969	1,105	291	152	918	370	0	1,943	6,748
15	1,969	1,048	291	227	1,109	370	0	1,943	6,956
16	2,302	1,048	291	227	1,109	370	0	1,943	7,290
17	2,302	1,048	291	227	1,109	370	0	1,943	7,290
18	2,302	1,048	291	227	969	370	0	1,943	7,150
TOTAL	31,913	15,209	5,144	2,303	13,433	2,897	52,029	36,998	159,927

The cost of raising a girl to age 18

Age	Food	Clothing	Health care	Personal care	Recreation, reading, gifts, school needs	Transportation	Child care	Shelter, furnishings, household operation	Total
Infant	1,274	1,679	206	0	0	0	4,363	1,928	9,450
1	997	515	206	87	394	0	5,963	2,006	10,169
2	1,080	497	206	87	394	0	4,988	1,975	9,226
3	1,080	497	277	87	394	0	4,988	1,943	9,265
4	1,479	505	277	87	394	0	4,988	1,943	9,672
5	1,479	505	277	87	486	44	4,988	1,943	9,808
6	1,479	681	277	83	567	44	3,626	1,943	8,699
7	1,510	681	277	83	794	44	3,626	1,943	8,958
8	1,510	681	277	83	794	44	3,626	1,943	8,958
9	1,510	706	277	83	794	44	3,626	1,943	8,983
10	1,641	706	277	83	794	44	3,626	1,943	9,114
11	1,641	706	277	83	794	44	3,626	1,943	9,114
12	1,641	1,166	291	260	811	370	0	1,943	6,482
13	1,721	1,166	291	260	811	370	0	1,943	6,561
14	1,721	1,166	291	260	918	370	0	1,943	6,669
15	1,721	1,199	291	326	1,109	370	0	1,943	6,959
16	1,721	1,199	291	326	1,109	370	0	1,943	6,959
17	1,721	1,199	291	326	1,109	370	0	1,943	6,959
18	1,721	1,199	291	326	969	370	0	1,943	6,768
TOTAL	28,648	16,656	5,144	3,020	13,433	2,897	52,029	36,998	158,826

Source: Centre for International Statistics at the Canadian Council on Social Development.

Another study, by the Vanier Institute of the Family, revealed that it costs about 15 percent of what the average middle-class family earns to care for one child, 25 percent to care for two children, and 33 percent for three or more children.

If you find these Canadian figures alarming, you may want to count your lucky stars that you're not an American parent! Here are some even scarier statistics from south of the border:

- The U.S. Department of Agriculture estimates that an ordinary middle-class family will spend approximately $176,420 U.S. to raise a child and pay for her college education. For higher-income families, the total is a wallet-popping $347,000 U.S. (Clearly, those designer togs and high-priced educational toys really add up over time!)

- *U.S. News and World Report* estimates that it can cost as much as $1.4 million U.S. to raise a child to age 18. (Of course, you have to take these particular figures with a grain of salt: the journalist who wrote the article in question factored in "acquisition costs" of up to $50,000 to cover the costs of infertility treatments for couples who are having difficulty conceiving and $1 million in forgone wages for time that one or both parents missed from work for family-related reasons!)

Does this mean that only the wealthiest of couples can afford to have children? That you should be prepared to slap your T4 on the table when you go to see your doctor for a preconception checkup to prove to the world that you've got the financial resources to raise a child?

Hardly.

What the statistics also fail to point out is that it is possible to juggle your budget and lifestyle around to provide for the needs of your growing family. If, for example, you or your partner decides to stay at home to raise your children for at least the first few years, you can chalk up some significant savings in the childcare column. Similarly, if you borrow baby items or shop second-hand, you can bring that first-year clothing figure down considerably.

The statistics also fail to tell you how to adjust for the costs associated with second and subsequent children. While you may spend a small fortune on baby gear for your first-born, any other children you have will be able to reuse much of that equipment. Unless you're blessed with triplets who each require their own car seat and high chair at the same time, you can figure that second and subsequent children aren't going to cost you quite as much as their older brother or sister. These economies of scale carry over to other budget lines as well: certain costs, like shelter, are unlikely to double if you have two children as opposed to just one—unless, of course, you decide to move out of your tiny bachelor apartment and into a 3,000-square-foot monster home!

Finally, there's the fact that you aren't expected to cough up the entire $160,000 at once. If you were, the birthrate would be next to zero! Even if you take the figures at face value and assume that you are going to spend $160,000 on each child over the next 18 years, it's important to keep in mind that you're only talking about an extra $170 per week—a much less frightening figure.

The moral of the story? There's enough to worry about when you're a parent. Don't let statistics like this make you crazy! Instead, read this book, arm yourself with the facts, and stop panicking about where the $160,000 is going to come from.

In 1996, children under age 15 made up 20.5 percent of the total Canadian population—up 3.7 percent from 1991 but down 29.6 percent since 1971.
Source: *The Financial Post Magazine.*

Two

Till Debt Do Us Part

Despite what many people believe, it's not those late third-trimester shopping trips that do in the budgets of many new parents (although, frankly, those weekly trips to Toys-R-Us don't exactly help!): it's the fact that many parents—particularly first-time parents—forget to adjust their spending habits to reflect the fact that their financial situation has changed.

As I noted in the previous chapter, new parents often find themselves faced with a double-edged sword: at the very time when their expenses are skyrocketing, one partner or the other ends up sacrificing a paycheque to take some time off work to care for the new arrival. In some cases, the decision to stay home with baby is temporary; in others, it's permanent. Either way, the family budget can take a significant hit.

Money Talk

"Communicate. Make sure your partner understands where you're coming from and has a good idea of your comfort zone when it comes to financial matters."
- *Kristin, 30, mother of one.*

That's something that Melinda and Robert, both 33, discovered for themselves when he switched jobs while she was pregnant with their second child. "There was a large adjustment in salary, and gone were any bonuses and benefits such as drug and dental plans," she recalls. "We found that we had to use credit cards to pay for anything other than mortgages, utilities, and groceries. Diapers, shampoo, and similar items were all purchased with a credit card. Needless to say, we found ourselves with a large credit card debt. We solved our problem, not overnight, but by gradually learning how to trim our expenses and by putting any lump sum of money that we received against our credit card balance."

Cindy, 40, and John, 42, experienced similar financial difficulties after Cindy changed careers following the birth of their twins five years ago.

Faced with the choice of commuting two hours each way or setting up her own business so that she could spend more time with her young family, Cindy decided to leave her high-paying job in the big city to take a shot at entrepreneurship.

Like most entrepreneurs, Cindy found that it took a while for her business to start turning a profit—something that led to a major financial crunch for her and John. Because Cindy was and still is the sole breadwinner for the household—John is unable to work because of a disability—the family's lifestyle took a nose-dive. They began relying on credit to get by. The result? An extraordinary amount of debt. Cindy and John have spent the past few years trying to get back on their feet financially. "We have lost almost everything we worked for in the past," Cindy admits. "But budgeting, changing our lifestyle, and really coming to terms with how we spend our money has helped us to solve our financial problems. More planning and less spending have been the keys to turning things around."

Facts and Figures

In 1993, 378,000 Canadian couples married or began to live together. That same year, 253,000 couples separated.

For richer and for poorer

While Cindy and John experienced tremendous stress as a result of their financial difficulties, unlike many couples they managed to refrain from blaming one another for the mess they found themselves in, choosing to focus instead on finding shared solutions to their money woes. "You can't take it out on each other: you need to just work at making it better," Cindy insists. "Our attitude was, 'We made the decision to spend the money as we did, so now we both have to be responsible for regaining lost ground.'"

A lot of couples could learn a lesson or two from Cindy and John. According to a recent U.S. study, seven out of ten couples fight about money on a regular basis. The problem, according to University of Denver psychology professor Howard Markham, who was interviewed for a recent article in *Money*, is that arguments about money frequently mask deeper problems in the relationship: "For most couples, money represents power, status, and self-worth. The hidden agenda is really who controls whom. Too often, talks about money turn into a test of wills rather than a rational discussion about goals."

Facts and Figures

According to a recent study conducted by *Working Mother* magazine, it is the female partner who assumes responsibility for managing the family's finances in two-thirds of dual-income households.

The financial tug of war is more likely to be a problem for couples in which both partners have radically different spending styles: if, for example, one partner is a natural-born saver and the other considers credit cards to be the eighth wonder of the world.

Are you and your partner financial soulmates?

Money tends to be one of those issues that is seldom discussed until after the honeymoon is over. And for good reason: It's a lot easier to ignore many of the less-than-flattering characteristics of your beloved before you're living under the same roof!

You might, of course, get a few hints about your partner's financial style while you're dating. Perhaps his idea of a hot date involves picking up empty beer bottles in parks so that he can turn them in at the beer store and collect the refunds! (Think I'm kidding? I know a couple who did this on a regular basis. Fortunately, they both thought it was an enjoyable—and profitable—way to spend an afternoon at the park.) Or maybe his idea of fun is spending the night on the town, buying rounds of drinks for all his friends so that he can impress everyone with his generosity.

While you might find yourself feeling mildly annoyed by your partner's spending habits before you start living under the same roof, for the most part the rose-coloured glasses don't come off until the honeymoon is long since behind you—typically when you and your partner are faced with your first major financial decision, such as whether to buy a house or have a baby. That's when it becomes obvious for the very first time to what extent your financial styles are compatible (see Table 2.1).

Table 2.1: Quiz: Are you financially compatible?

Wondering if you and your partner are financial soulmates or whether your financial styles are about as compatible as oil and water? Here's a quick way to find out. Place a checkmark under the "Me" column for a particular statement if you agree with it. Place a checkmark under the "My partner" column if you think your partner would agree with it. (Better yet, let him or her answer this part of the quiz!) When you're finished responding to all of the statements, you'll have an idea how closely your answers match up.

Family Finance

	Me	My partner
I spend a lot of time worrying about money.	_____	_____
I have a pretty good idea of our net worth at any given time.	_____	_____
I hate owing money to anyone, including the bank. I wish we were debt free.	_____	_____
A penny spent on interest payments is a penny wasted.	_____	_____
I don't like to carry an outstanding balance on my credit card.	_____	_____
One of my goals is to be mortgage-free as soon as possible.	_____	_____
I don't mind doing without certain things if it means we can save some money.	_____	_____
I think through my purchases carefully. I'm not an impulse buyer.	_____	_____
Having a nest egg set aside makes me feel secure.	_____	_____
I typically use my income tax refund to get ahead financially (e.g. paying off debts).	_____	_____
Money isn't much of a worry to me.	_____	_____
I have no idea what my net worth is, nor do I particularly care.	_____	_____
Debt doesn't bother me all that much. Money is a tool to get the things you want in life.	_____	_____
I'd rather spend money on interest charges than postpone a purchase indefinitely.	_____	_____
I don't mind owing money on my credit card if it means I'm able to purchase the things I want.	_____	_____
I'm not in any particular rush to pay off my mortgage. I'd rather use the money for other things.	_____	_____
I hate depriving myself of things I want in order to save money.	_____	_____
If I see a great deal on something, I want to buy it right then and there. Why wait?	_____	_____
Knowing that I can borrow money if I need it makes me feel secure.	_____	_____
I typically use my income tax refund to purchase things I want.	_____	_____

The first 10 statements are the types of things a saver would say. The next 10 are the kinds of statements that a spender would make. Are you and your partner savers, spenders, or are you each a little of both? (Hint: Some people act like savers in some situations and spenders in other situations.) How compatible are your financial styles?

So what do you do if you discover that you and your partner have radically different spending styles? Part ways? Agree to disagree? Try to find some financial middle ground?

It depends.

If the rest of your relationship is solid, you've got a strong incentive to try to find ways to repair the financial trouble spots. If, on the other hand, you're fighting about sex, conflicting career goals, and everything else under the sun, perhaps there isn't much of a relationship left to save.

This was certainly the case for Christine, 24, a single mother of one, and her former partner: "Nine months after the birth of our child, my partner and I separated. One of the reasons was finances. My partner still lived life to the fullest. He was a waiter who did not save money, still bought luxury items without thought to the future, and never gave thought to future expenses that would overwhelm us. I tried to save money, but did not have control over him. Controlling someone else's spending habits is next to impossible since you can't have the money police follow them around all the time."

Money Talk

"Set up three different bank accounts—one for each partner and one for the household."
- *Cindy, 40, mother of two.*

Other couples go through an initial period of adjustment when they first set up house together.

"My husband and I were young when we got married and we had very different spending habits," admits Krista, a 32-year-old mother of one. "I must say I nagged him constantly and I would get very angry, but with time I just gave up. He eventually learned how his free-spending habits were hurting us and he slowly changed his ways by himself. In the beginning, he made me carry all the money and he only used his credit card for gas. Today, he is very careful of his spending. My husband and I are now a great financial team, but it took us a long time to get to this point."

"It was hard for a couple of years," adds Carolyn, a 35-year-old mother of three, whose partner, Doug, had a tendency to overspend during the early years of their marriage. "I would have to be the 'enforcer,' which is not a fun role. I would get completely exasperated when I was trying to save 25 cents on something and he would be spending constantly."

"This has been, and to a degree still is, a major issue for us," says Fiona, a 32-year-old mother of six. "We have had many disagreements and hard times in our marriage because of our initially opposing views on money and its purpose. By setting goals together while keeping each person's individual needs in mind, we were able to come up with a strategy that has allowed us to have some freedom in spending, while at the same time pursuing our dreams."

The fact that you have different spending habits doesn't have to spell doomsday for your relationship, however. Many couples find ways to work around the problem.

Show Me the Money!

"Allow the one who is the stronger saver to handle the finances, and have the spender try to put some control on their urges, even if that means going on a weekly allowance. In the end, it all comes down to how badly you both want financial success. If it's important, sacrifices have to be made in the short-term. You can't just live for today, paycheque to paycheque."
- *Paul, 34, awaiting the birth of his second child.*

"We are definitely different in our spending habits," explains Laura, a 22-year-old mother of one. "My husband likes to spend his money and I like to make sure our bills get paid before anything else! In order to help him stop spending, I control the money. If he would like money to spend on the extras, he asks if we have enough money and I answer him honestly."

"Jeff and I have different spending habits," adds Kristin, a 30-year-old mother of one. "He tends to be more of a free spender and is more optimistic about our financial situation. He's also a lot more comfortable with debt than I am. While I'm not a big saver, I tend to be more conservative and prefer to incur as little debt as possible. It's a struggle, but by talking things through we can usually come to a compromise we both can live with."

"My husband loves to spend money on his hobby, sports card collecting, and I do not have a hobby that is expensive, so I sometimes resent the fact that he takes a fair bit of our money and puts it toward buying sports cards," admits Stephanie, a 26-year-old mother of one. "We've learned to compromise about this issue. We ensure that all of the bills are taken care of and that we've contributed to our savings and spent some money on the family before he can spend any money on his hobby."

"My husband and I have very different spending habits," notes Diane, a 29-year-old mother of two. "I am the spender and he is the saver. This does tend to be an issue because I like to 'get my money's worth.' I believe you get what you pay for, which means I don't always buy the cheapest item available. He likes to buy the cheapest one no matter what. We haven't come to a magic solution yet. We just try to compromise as much as possible."

Money Talk

"We are fortunate in that we have very similar approaches to money. We've also always earned very similar wages, so that creates a sense of equality."
- *Louise, 28, mother of one.*

Couples in which both partners have a tendency to overspend often find it difficult to discipline themselves to make the best financial choices. "My husband and I are both spenders," admits Jackie, a 31-year-old mother of two. "We do save—we make RRSP contributions and we're saving for our children's education, and so on—but not nearly as much as we could and should. I am responsible for the finances in our house and I tend to get stressed when I pay the bills each month. I will rant for a few days about how we must do this and that better with our money, but it never seems to happen." So even though there may be some occasional sparring involved if you and your partner don't see eye to eye on financial matters, the fact that one of you is a saver could be a blessing in disguise.

The dirty little secret

Contrary to popular belief, it's not just overspenders who can find themselves experiencing serious money problems. If you're in the habit of living from paycheque to paycheque—and frankly a lot of Canadians are!—you could find yourself being blown out of the water financially by one of life's little curve balls such as a job loss or an unplanned pregnancy.

Krista, 32, and Vincent, 34, found themselves facing a financial crisis shortly before their son was born. Krista explains: "When my husband and I lost our jobs due to downsizing and a plant closing only a couple of months before Ryan was due, I really didn't know what we were going to do. Fortunately, we lived in a small house, we had been saving our money, we already knew how to live on a budget, and we had a loving, supportive family who were there when we needed their help. We made it through a lot better than some others at my husband's plant. Many people lost their homes and eventually their marriages. They just couldn't hold it together financially or emotionally."

Darla, 38, and Marvin, 40, the parents of five children, found themselves faced with a similar crisis when they were hit with two real estate losses over a short period of time. Darla explains, "It started when my husband took a job in another city 400 km away. We had to sell our home and ended up taking a loss of $35,000. Then we sold a piece of land that we owned and took another loss of $55,000. I started using credit cards to get over some humps and one thing led to another and we ended up in a snowball situation. We eventually had to take a second mortgage out on our home because I was having some serious medical problems like panic attacks and migraine headaches because of the stress of the financial situation. We are now on the right track again and I am happy to say that we no longer have any credit cards to get us in trouble again. We pay cash for everything so our spending is mostly under control."

Money problems like these couples faced are more common than you might think. Each year, one out of every two hundred Canadian families files for bankruptcy. The problem is that no one wants to talk about it. Sex may be a perfectly acceptable topic for conversation, but money problems continue to be treated like every family's dirty little secret.

the Bottom line

When Carolyn and Doug, both 35, hit the debt wall a few years ago, they were forced to change their spending habits overnight. "We cut back on everything," recalls Carolyn, a mother of three. "No meals or coffees out, no magazines, no cable, we used the library instead of buying books, and my husband started bringing his lunch to work. I always had plenty of groceries in the house, so we couldn't use the excuse that there was nothing to make for dinner and decide to eat out instead. The most effective way for us to cut our expenses simply was not to carry much money."

How financially fit is your family?

According to a recent study conducted on behalf of consulting firm Deloitte & Touche, Canadians spend an average of only five hours a year planning their finances. While the majority of us seem satisfied to let our finances take care of themselves, the experts recommend that we put a lot more time and effort into coming up with a financial game plan.

Of course, it's hard to figure out where you're headed and how you're going to get there if you don't have an idea where you are right now. If you've never sat down and taken a financial snapshot of your family, there's no time like the present to do so! You can use the tools on the following pages to calculate your net worth (Table 2.2) and to analyze your income and expenses (Table 2.3)—two important indicators of your family's overall financial well-being.

Note: if you prefer a high-tech approach to number crunching, you can either use one of the many excellent personal finance software packages available for this purpose or use one of the online financial calculators available at iMoney (**www.imoney.com**) and Quicken (**www.quicken.ca**) as well as at the Web sites of most of the major chartered banks.

Table 2.2: Net worth
ASSETS

Possessions

House _____

Other real estate _____

Car _____

Household furnishings _____

Electronic and computer equipment _____

Jewellery _____

Other _____

Savings and investments

Bank accounts _____

Canada Savings Bonds _____

Term deposits and GICs _____

Employee savings plans _____

Life insurance cash value _____

Stocks _____

Bonds _____

Mutual funds _____

Educational savings plans _____

Retirement savings

Registered retirement savings plans _____

continued...

Table 2.2: Net worth

ASSETS

Possessions	
Savings accounts	_____
GICs	_____
Stocks	_____
Bonds	_____
Mutual funds	_____
Pension plan	_____

LIABILITIES

Personal debts (be sure to include the balance owing and the interest rate charged for any loans or credit cards)

Mortgage	_____
Car loan	_____
Credit card balances	_____
Personal loans	_____

LIABILITIES

Lines of credit	_____
Unpaid bills (e.g., utility or phone bills)	_____
Income tax owing	_____
Money owed to relatives	_____
Other debts	_____
Investment debts	
Investment loans	_____
Business loans	_____
Other debts	_____
Total debts	_____

NET WORTH

What you own	_____
Less what you owe	_____
Your net worth	_____

Analyzing your net worth statement

While the bottom line on your net worth statement is important—it tells you whether you own more than you owe or vice versa—you can learn a whole lot more from it than just that. Here's what to look for and how you might want to respond (see Table 2.3):

Table 2.3: Making sense of your net worth statement

If your net worth statement shows that...	You might want to...
You have an excessive amount of debt	Focus on debt reduction
You have a large outstanding balance on your credit cards	Consider applying for a lower-interest debt consolidation loan and cutting up your credit cards
You're paying a high interest rate on your credit card	Consider paying for a "no frills" credit card with a lower interest rate. (You can compare credit card rates by visiting the financial tools section of the iMoney Web site (**www.imoney.com**)
You're paying a high rate of interest on your mortgage or other loans	Consider refinancing your mortgage and other loans at a lower rate unless, of course, your financial institution charges a huge penalty for doing so
You have money sitting in your savings account or in Canada Savings Bonds as well as a large amount of debt	Use as much of your savings as possible to pay down your debts
You have a large amount of money sitting in a chequing account that is earning little or no interest	Find a chequing or savings account that pays a higher rate of interest on your money. You might even consider a T-bill or money-market account.
You don't have an emergency fund that equals three to six months' worth of net income.	Make it a priority to start building up a nest egg so you won't be caught off guard if you lose your job or find yourself faced by some other financial curve ball

Wondering how your family's income stacks up to that of other Canadian families? Here are some figures from *The Money Companion*, by Elaine Wyatt, that will let you know how well you're keeping up with the Joneses!

- The wealthiest 20 percent of Canadian families earn more than $80,000 per year.
- The next wealthiest 20 percent of Canadian families take home between $57,793 and $80,000

- The next 40 percent of Canadian families—"average Canadians"—earn between $25,820 and $57,793 per year.
- The poorest 20 percent of Canadian families have incomes of less than $25,820 per year.

Now that you've had the chance to size up your financial net worth at this point, you should take a moment to consider how you're doing on a month-to-month basis by analyzing your cash flow. In other words, is your income great than your expenses, or vice versa?

Table 2.4: Income vs. expenses

Enter the monthly amount for each category.

INCOME

Your employment income	_____
Your partner's employment income	_____
Bonuses	_____
Investment income	_____
Rental income	_____
Spousal support	_____
Child support	_____
Other sources of income	_____
Total Income	_____

EXPENSES

Taxes and other income deductions	
Income tax	_____
Canada/Quebec pension plan	_____
Company pension plan contributions	_____
Employment Insurance premiums	_____
Union dues	_____
Other deductions	_____
Household expenses	
Rent or mortgage	_____
Property taxes	_____
House insurance	_____
Utilities (heat, hydro, water)	_____

continued...

Table 2.4: Income vs. expenses

Service contracts (cleaning, lawn care, snow removal, etc.)   _____

Telephone   _____

Cable TV   _____

Household equipment   _____

Household repair   _____

Taxes and other income deductions

Other   _____

EXPENSES

Food

Groceries   _____

Restaurant meals and takeout food   _____

Other   _____

Transportation

Car loan payments   _____

Gasoline   _____

Maintenance/repairs   _____

License fees (vehicle and driver's license)   _____

Car insurance   _____

Tolls and parking fees   _____

Bus, subway, or commuter train fares   _____

Taxis   _____

Other   _____

Personal care

Clothing   _____

Dry cleaning   _____

Hair salon   _____

Health club membership   _____

Other   _____

Debt repayment

Credit cards   _____

Line of credit   _____

Student loans   _____

Other debts   _____

Entertainment

continued...

Table 2.4: Income vs. expenses

Movies	_____
Concerts	_____
Vacations	_____
Gifts	_____
Books	_____

EXPENSES

Taxes and other income deductions	
Video rentals	_____
Hobbies	_____
Wine, beer, and other alcoholic beverages	_____
Other	_____
Professional services	
Accountant	_____
Lawyer	_____
Financial advisor	_____
Health care	
Drugs	_____
Dental care	_____
Eye care	_____
Other	_____
Educational expenses	
Tuition	_____
Books	_____
Other	
Insurance	
Life insurance	_____
Disability insurance	_____
Medical insurance	_____
Other expenses	_____
Childcare	_____
Charitable donations	_____
Other	
Total Expenses	_____

Analyzing your income and expenses

The purpose of an income and expenses statement is to take a snapshot of your financial situation by figuring out how much money is coming in and how much money is going out. This task will be a whole lot easier if you're the kind of person who keeps detailed financial records. If you're not, you'll have your work cut out for you as you try your hand at forensic accounting!

You don't have to be a rocket scientist to interpret an income and expense statement. It's pretty obvious whether you're dealing with good news or bad. Here's what you might discover as you work through this particular exercise—and how you might want to change your financial strategies, depending on what you find:

Table 2.5: Making sense of your income and expenses statement

If your cash flow statement shows...	You might want to...
You are spending more money than you are bringing in	Look for ways to boost your income and/or to cut your spending so that you end up with at least a small surplus of money at the end of each month
You are spending an excessive amount of money on certain types of expenditures (e.g., entertainment, dining out, clothing) than your income allows	Look for ways to cut back your spending in these areas without sacrificing your lifestyle altogether
You are spending a significant amount of money simply servicing your debts	Start working on paying off your credit cards, line of credits, car loans, mortgage, and other loans

Meet Joe and Jane Average

Now that you've had a chance to engage in some heavy-duty financial navel-gazing, you might be interested to find out how your family's financial situation measures up to that of the "average" Canadian household—whatever that means! The most recent figures from Statistics Canada are summarized in Table 2.6.

Table 2.6: Average household expenditures, 1997

Personal income taxes	$10,634
Shelter	9,869
Transportation	6,204
Food	5,703
Personal insurance payments and pension contributions	2,783
Recreation	2,780
Household operation	2,284
Clothing	2,182
Household furnishings and equipment	1,335
Gifts of money and contributions	1,240
Health care	1,153
Tobacco products and alcoholic beverages	1,139
Miscellaneous	796
Personal care	664
Education	659
Reading materials and other printed matter	275
Games of chance (e.g., lottery tickets)	247
Total	**$49,947**

Source: Statistics Canada.

As you can see, income taxes and housing costs eat up approximately 40 percent of the average Canadian family's budget. Other significant expenditures include transportation and food.

If your spending on one of these budget lines seems to be way out of whack—if, for example, your household income is around $50,000, but you're spending more than $8,000 on recreation—you might want to look for some ways to reduce your expenses. (Hint: You'll find plenty of money-saving tips in Chapter 8.) The logical first step is to put your family on a budget.

Now before you run screaming from the room, allow me to have my say about budgets. I agree that there are a lot more fun things to do with your time than camping out at the kitchen table and trying to come up with a game plan for your spending, and that it can be a little tedious to track your spending day after day. Unfortunately, budgets are a necessary evil, an unavoidable aspect of money management like paying your bills and filing your tax return.

Don't get me wrong: writing a budget doesn't have to be a test of endurance, nor does sticking to it have to be an exercise in deprivation. Not if you're smart about it, anyway. Here are some tips on writing a budget that you can actually live with.

- **Decide what you hope to achieve by following a budget.** Are you hoping to eliminate your credit card debts? Save for a holiday? Or build up your emergency savings account? You're more likely to stick with your budget if you've got some concrete goals in mind.

- **Reach for your calculator.** Pull out your income and expense statement and rework it so that it will help you to achieve your financial goals. Want to take the kids on a trip to Disney World next winter? Better start setting aside some money every week so you'll be able to afford that rendezvous with Mickey. Hoping to pay off your car loan this year? Look for other areas of your budget where you can cut back a little, and then apply this "found money" against the balance of your car loan each month.

- **Look at the big picture.** Going on a crash weight-loss diet doesn't work. Neither does going on a crash money diet. Rather than going for the "quick fix" in an effort to eliminate your debt or build up your savings overnight, come up with a budget that you can stick with over the long run.

- **Get other family members to buy into the plan.** There's no point coming up with a budget if you're the only one who's prepared to stick to it. That's why it's important to get your partner and your children involved in setting the budget. Obviously, you won't be lecturing your one-year-old about the evils of spending more than you earn, but it's a lesson that older children can certainly be taught! (You'll find lots of tips on teaching kids about money elsewhere in this book.)

- **Keep it simple.** Rather than spending hours trying to account for every nickel and dime, settle for keeping track of the big chunks of money. Does it really matter whether the $20 you had in your pocket was spent on five magazines or fifteen takeout coffees? Not unless you've got a Type A++ personality or you're someone with a lot of time on your hands! Just log the expense as $20 for "spending money" and you'll save yourself and those around you a lot of grief.

- **Realize that you're going to fall off the wagon from time to time.** Everyone does. The secret is to get back on as soon as possible—not to abandon your budget entirely and go on the ultimate spending spree, figuring that since you've already blown it, you might as well shop 'till you drop. Remember, it's a lot less painful to cope with a $200 financial *faux pas* than a $5,000 budget blowout.

The perils of plastic

You've no doubt noticed a recurring theme in this chapter: the evils of credit cards! I'm not going to try to pretend that credit cards don't have a lot to offer: they're an excellent source of free credit (provided you pay off your balance in full each month, and you aren't tempted to take a cash advance) and they offer a safe and convenient alternative to carrying large amounts of cash.

Of course, like almost everything else in life, credit cards do have their dark side. While we all like to think that we do a good job of handling our credit cards, the fact remains that only half of Canadians manage to pay off the balances in full each month.

Here are some other rather damning facts about credit cards:

- According to Elaine Wyatt, author of *The Money Companion,* in October 1997, Canadians owed $20.5 billion on their Mastercard and Visa cards alone—$1.8 billion more than they owed in the fall of 1995.
- The average Canadian has three credit cards—significantly less than the four to five credit cards that find their way into the wallet of the typical American, but more than the one to two credit card maximum that the money experts generally advise.
- In 1995, there were 28.8 million credit cards in circulation in Canada— a 4.7 percent increase over 1994, according to Jim Carroll and Rick Broadhead, authors of *Canadian Money Management Online.*
- According to Industry Canada, there were 840 million Visa and Mastercard transactions carried out by Canadians in 1995—nearly 2.5 million transactions each day!

Facts and Figures

Think you've got too many credit cards? Imagine what it would be like to be Walter Cavanagh, a financial planner in Santa Clara, California, who turned up in the 1998 *Guinness Book of Records* with 1,397 credit cards and a total credit limit of $1.65 million U.S. You've got to wonder what Walter's clients have to say about that.
Source: *The Globe and Mail.*

How to avoid getting in trouble with credit cards

What the numbers don't tell you, of course, is how incredibly seductive credit cards can be. It's easy to forget that you're spending "real" money when there aren't any bills and coins changing hands. It's also easy to lose track of how many $40 purchases you've made over the course of a month until a $1,000 credit card bill shows up on your doorstep.

As with anything else in life, when it comes to managing your credit cards, an ounce of prevention is worth a pound of cure. Here are some tips on avoiding credit card problems:

Keep track of your credit card slips so that you can compare them against your monthly statement. If you notice any errors, contact your credit card company immediately and ask them to investigate.

- **Limit the number of credit cards you use.** The more cards you have, the more likely you'll be tempted to use them. Rather than carrying around a wallet full of department store and gas company credit cards, stick with one or two major credit cards.

- **Ask your bank to chop your credit limit.** Credit card companies love nothing more than to "reward" good customers by raising their credit limits. (Any why not? They're in the business of making money! If you've got a couple of thousand dollars worth of room on your credit card, you might be tempted to dash out and buy that home theatre system you've been drooling over for years.) More often than not, you don't even have to request a credit limit increase. It just happens. You get a congratulatory letter from your credit card company, letting you know that they've topped up your credit limit with an extra couple of thousand dollars, or you happen to notice that the credit limit that appears on your credit card statement has doubled or tripled since the last time you checked. If you don't want to be tempted to overspend just because the credit card company is willing to lend you more money, then pick up that phone and decline this "opportunity" to dig yourself into a financial hole.

- **Switch from a credit card to a charge card.** Visa and Mastercard are credit cards: you're only required to make a token payment each month to keep your account in good standing. American Express, on the other hand, is a charge card: you're expected to pay off the balance in full each month. While there's no guarantee that you'll stick to the financial high road just because you're carrying an American Express card around in your wallet, you'll be less likely to overspend if you know you're supposed to write a cheque for the total owing at the end of the month. Note: American Express also offers a regular credit card, the Optima card.

- **Beware of department store credit cards.** They tend to charge extremely high interest rates—sometimes as high as 28.8 percent. Avoid these cards like the plague if you tend to carry an outstanding balance.
- **Think about what you're buying on credit.** It's one thing to buy a fax machine for your small business on credit: with any luck, that purchase will help to put money back in your pocket. It's quite another to borrow money so that you can live beyond your means—and, whether you're prepared to admit it to yourself or not, that's exactly what you're doing if you carry an unpaid credit card balance that is largely made up of restaurant meals, purchases at the liquor store, and other goods that have long since been consumed. (Besides, who wants to be paying interest on a night on the town six months after the fact!)

the Bottom line

Those "buy now, pay later" promotions are another form of credit that can get you into trouble. Take advantage of these programs only if they include interest-free loans and you have the necessary funds in your bank account right now. Throw the money into a term deposit or write it out of your cheque register so you forget you have it—you'll still have the money to pay off the loan when it comes due and you'll earn interest on your money in the meantime. Otherwise, you will pay interest from the day of purchase. Talk about a "no money miracle"! One other thing to note: The "financing charge" that applies to many of these promotions can amount to more than you would pay in interest over the course of an entire year. That's no bargain!

How much debt is too much debt?

Here's a lesson that many families learn the hard way: there's a world of difference between the amount of money that the banks are willing to lend you and the amount of debt that you feel comfortable carrying.

Don't understand what I'm talking about? Let me explain.

Financial institutions look at your total debt-service ratio to determine whether or not you can handle any more debt. This total, which is based on your gross monthly income (your income before taxes), represents your total debt payments plus your housing costs.

Money Talk

The term *gross debt-service ratio* refers to the percentage of your monthly income that financial institutions are willing to lend you to purchase a home (usually 30 to 32 percent). Your total debt-service ratio, on the other hand, is the total amount of debt you are carrying: your housing costs plus all your consumer debt (e.g., loans, credit cards, lines of credit, and more).

Example:

Gross monthly income	$4,000
Total debt-service ratio of 40%	$1,600
Mortgage payments	$1,100
Credit cards	$150
Car payments	$350

Someone who grosses $4,000 per month would be allowed to carry $1,600 worth of payments each month: enough to cover a $1,100 mortgage payment, a $350 car loan, and a $150 credit card payment. (Watch out! The credit card payment is the minimum payment required on your card, not the total amount that you charge. It's not difficult to see how much trouble you could find yourself in if you gave your credit card even a modest work-out. In fact, if you wanted to pay your credit card off in full each month and yet still stay within the 40 percent total debt-service ratio zone, you wouldn't be able to charge more than $150 each month.)

Now let's look at the fine print. Something the financial institutions often fail to explain is the fact that they throw your entire credit card limit into the calculation, not just the amount that you have charged at any given time. If, for example, you have a credit card with a $5,000 credit limit and you're required to pay off 3 percent of the balance each month, that's $150 of your gross debt-service ratio used up even if the credit card never actually leaves your wallet! If you have a couple of credit cards and a line of credit, you could find a huge chunk of your gross debt-service ratio being gobbled up, even if you never use any of these sources of instant credit. The solution? Close as many of your unused credit accounts as possible if you want to free up some room in your total debt-service ratio.

Another thing that the financial institutions don't tell you is how it feels to be living with a total debt-service ratio of 40 percent. I can tell you from personal experience that it's not a whole lot of fun. At one point in our lives, we had a huge mortgage, two car loans, three major charge cards, and two lines of credit. Our monthly payments were eating up a good 40 percent of our paycheques each month. The bank seemed to think this was a reasonable amount of debt for a young couple with three children to be carrying. We learned the hard way that it wasn't.

Show Me the Money!

Here's a painless way to ensure that you always have the necessary funds on hand for those large bills that only show up once a year, such as property taxes and car insurance. Add up the amount of money you spend on these types of bills and then divide the total by 52. This is the amount of money you need to set aside each week to make sure that you've got enough money on hand when the bills come due. If you think you might be tempted to use these funds for a less noble purpose, keep them in a separate savings account.

The warning signs that you're headed for financial trouble

Financial difficulties can sneak up on you and catch you unaware. One minute you're on solid financial ground—or at least you think you are! The next, you're dodging phone calls from creditors and wondering how things could go so wrong so quickly.

It's all too easy to ignore the warning signs that you're headed for money trouble. After all, who wants to even consider the possibility that they could be flirting with financial disaster? Often, it's easier to convince yourself that things going to be all right—"We've got a good income, so there's really no problem"—than it is to face up to the fact that you're overloaded with debts and sinking fast.

That's why it's important to take realistic stock of your financial situation on a regular basis—to take a good hard look at your spending habits, warts and all. If you know that your money management habits place you somewhere between saint and sinner, but you're not quite sure which way you're leaning, try your hand at the quiz in Table 2.7.

Table 2.7: Quiz: Are you headed for financial trouble?

Do you know how to spot the warning signs that you're headed for financial trouble? The following quiz should help you to decide if it's time to put away your credit cards for a while. Check off the statements that apply to your situation and then tally up your total to find out how well you're doing in heading off the financial storm clouds.

_____ I frequently end up paying my bills after they are past due.

_____ I'm bouncing cheques on a regular basis.

_____ I am getting further in debt with each passing month.

_____ I find myself dipping into my savings in order to come up with enough money to pay my bills.

_____ I have used an advance from one credit card to make the minimum payment on another card.

_____ Most months, I am only able to pay the minimum amount on my credit cards.

_____ At least one of my credit cards is over the limit.

_____ I frequently borrow money or use my credit card to pay for items that I previously bought with cash.

_____ I am receiving calls from collection agencies because of my overdue bills.

_____ I have put off spending money on prescription drugs, dental checkups, and car repairs because I can't afford them.

_____ My utilities have been cut off from time to time because I've been unable to pay my bills.

_____ If I lost my job (or my partner lost his/her job), we'd be in serious financial trouble right away.

_____ I have less than a month's income stashed away in my emergency fund.

_____ I've lost track of how much money I actually owe to my creditors.

_____ I have experienced problems with my partner because of my spending habits.

_____ Sometimes I find it hard to concentrate at work because I'm so worried about my debts.

_____ I feel depressed and hopeless when I think about my financial situation.

_____ I have given false information on at least one occasion in order to obtain credit.

_____ My wages have been garnisheed on at least one occasion to pay some of my outstanding debts.

_____ I am having difficulty sleeping because I'm worried about my financial situation.

If you checked off more than five of these statements, you're clearly headed for financial trouble. Don't think you're in the clear if you only checked off one or two statements, however. Take it as a wake-up call that it's time to pull up your financial socks and change the way you manage your money.

How to dig yourself out of a financial hole

If you took the quiz and discovered to your horror that you're in worse financial shape than you realized, you're probably wondering what you can do to turn your situation around. Here are a few ideas:

- **Pay off your most expensive debts first.** That means eliminating the balances on your department-store cards, gas cards, and credit cards (high interest-rate debt) before you try to finish paying off your line of credit, your car, or your mortgage (low interest-rate debt).

- **Consider getting a consolidation loan if it will help to decrease the amount of money you are spending on interest payments.** There's just one catch: this strategy can backfire if you start using your credit cards again. You have to promise yourself that you're going to put your credit cards away until you've finished paying off your consolidation loan—perhaps even cut them up altogether.

- **Look for pockets of cash that you can apply to your debts.** It doesn't make sense to have $2,000 sitting in your chequing account if you're paying 28.8 percent interest on a $2,000 balance of your credit card. While you might feel like you're doing something wrong by spending the small bit of cash you've managed to sock away over the years, in the end you'll be further ahead if you use it to reduce your debt. Here's how financial writer Tony Martin explained this point in *The Globe and Mail*: "Paying off that $2,000 balance on your department store card that's costing you 28.8 percent is the same as getting a guaranteed 28.8 percent return on an investment. By comparison, you'd have to find a guaranteed investment certificate paying 58 percent to do better on an after-tax basis." It's a pretty compelling argument, isn't it?

- **Get in the habit of saving before you spend.** While this may almost sound like blasphemy to anyone who has bought into the "buy now, pay later" advertising pitches, you'll save a small fortune in interest if you get in the habit of deferring major purchases until you have the necessary money sitting in your bank account. There's also an added bonus: you won't find yourself scrambling to find the money when it's finally time to pay the bill—something that could become a major problem if you were to lose your job in the meantime. If you're not a natural-born saver (and frankly, not many people are), you might find it easier to rely on forced savings methods, like signing up for a preauthorized contribution plan (PAC) to a mutual fund or a payroll deduction plan for Canada Savings Bonds, employee shares, or a group RRSP. The best savings plan, after all, is the one that you don't have to think about.

- **Learn how to anticipate expenses so that you don't get caught short of funds.** If your car is due for a brake job, set some money aside before you pay a visit to your friendly neighbourhood mechanic—not after the credit card bill is past due. Similarly, if your property taxes are due each March, start setting aside funds months in advance so that the money will be there when you need it. Then, instead of writing a cheque against your line of credit and paying interest on your property taxes, you'll be able to settle the bill with cash.

Money Talk

"Separating from my partner almost led to my bankruptcy, but I did not give in. After being refused a small loan to help get me back on my feet and being offered the alternative of bankruptcy, I realized that I would have to work some major miracles to pay off credit cards, car loans, and everyday expenses while supplying the little things that my child needed. I became a very frugal person. I also wasn't afraid to ask for help… Now I am doing much better financially. Everything is being paid on time and I no longer need my parents' help."
- *Christine, 24, single mother of one.*

- **If you like using a credit card because it's more convenient than carrying cash, start using a debit card instead.** Debit cards are as convenient as using a credit card, but you aren't left with a massive bill to pay at the end of the month.
- **Don't allow yourself to fall back into the hole again.** Cut up your credit cards so that you won't be tempted to run them up to their limit again. Be sure to contact the credit card issuer to officially close the account. Otherwise, you'll still be responsible for any charges that show up on your account. If you don't like the idea of getting rid of your credit cards entirely, store them in your safety deposit box at the bank or wrap them in plastic, drop them into a plastic container filled with water, and store the container in your freezer. (Hey, it's one way to put your spending habits on ice!)

What you don't know about your credit rating can hurt you

Here's a statistic that will make your hair stand on end: studies have shown that one in four credit files contains some sort of error. If it's a serious enough error, it could make it impossible for you to obtain credit until the error is corrected—convincing evidence that what you don't know about your credit rating can hurt you.

Your credit rating is established at the moment your first application for credit is approved, perhaps when you obtained your first credit card, arranged your first car loan, or bought some sort of electronic gizmo on the installment plan.

The way to establish a good credit rating is to borrow money and pay it back on time. If you don't, the word will get out that you're not a good credit risk—and bad news travels fast in credit-granting circles.

Here's something else you need to know: the bad news also sticks around for a very long time. If you miss a payment or are late with a payment, this fact will show up on your credit file for the next seven years. (And you thought that breaking mirrors was bad luck!)

Big Brother is watching you

Each month, your creditors are contacted by your local credit bureau and asked to report on your creditworthiness. The credit bureau collects data on your outstanding balance, whether or not you've missed any payments, and your current credit rating according to each of your creditors. This information is then recorded in your credit file so that it can be made available to prospective creditors the next time you apply for a loan.

Time and time again, each of your creditors assigns you a credit rating based on your credit history. Here's what the codes mean:

- "R" refers to your credit rating on revolving credit (e.g., credit cards in which you can pay as much or as little as you would like each month, as long as you make at least the minimum payment).
- "I" refers to your credit rating on installment credit (e.g., loans in which you make fixed payments on a predetermined schedule).
- "O" refers to your credit rating on open credit (e.g., cards such as American Express that require you to pay the balance in full each month).

You are then given a rating from 0 to 9 that indicates how responsibly you handle credit. Here's what some of those numbers signify:

- "0" means that you have been approved for credit, but you don't have a credit history yet, either because your credit was just approved or because you've never actually used the credit card that you applied for.
- "1" means that you pay your bills within 30 days.

- "2" means that you pay in 30 to 60 days and are a payment behind.
- "5" means that you take 120 days or more to pay and that your account is currently overdue.
- "9" means that a collection agency has been called in to try to obtain payment on your account.

The two components of your credit card rating are then matched up: You are assigned a rating of "R1" if you make your revolving credit payments within 30 days and a rating of "I2" if you pay your installment credit bills in 30 to 60 days and are currently a payment behind.

Not everything shows up on your credit rating, however. Delinquent student loans, unpaid tax bills, and missed rent payments are just a few of the things that don't get picked up by Big Brother.

Show Me the Money!

The Canadian Bankers Association recommends that you ask yourself the following four questions each time you're thinking about borrowing money: Is the item I am purchasing worth the cost I will actually pay by the end of the loan? What would happen if my financial situation were to change during the course of the loan? What impact will the decision to borrow have on my family? Can I afford credit?

How to check your credit rating

While the whole credit rating process sounds tremendously scientific, errors can and do occur. Back in 1991, CBC-TV's consumer show *Marketplace* sent people across the country into their local credit bureaus to obtain copies of their credit reports. Forty-seven percent of the people who participated in the study found errors on their credit reports—and in 13 percent of cases, these errors were serious enough to have resulted in credit application denials. That's why it's important to get in touch with your local credit bureau to find out what's involved in obtaining a copy of your credit rating.

Money Talk

If your local credit bureau happens to be Equifax Canada—a huge credit reporting company that has more than 80 percent of the market for consumer information in Canada—you can obtain a copy of your credit report by sending a copy of two pieces of signed identification, information about your current address, your former address, your date of birth, and your daytime phone number to Equifax Canada by mail at Equifax Canada, P.O. Box 190, Jean Talon Station, Montreal, Quebec. H1S 2Z2, or by fax at 1-800-363-4430. You should receive a credit report by mail within two to three weeks.

Once your credit report arrives, sit down and review it carefully to make sure that it's free of errors. If you find an error caused by one of your creditors (e.g., your credit card company has reported that you typically pay your bills in 120 days, but you've never been a day late with a payment in your life), you will need to get in touch with the creditor and ask them to contact the credit bureau to have the information corrected. If you find that your credit report contains information about someone else's credit situation—a horrifying but all-too-common occurrence—then you will need to provide whatever written proof you can and ask the credit bureau to investigate.

Don't forget about the situation once you've asked the credit bureau to investigate. Follow up and make sure that they take the appropriate actions to have your file modified and that anyone who requested credit information about you in the recent past has been notified about the errors, as required by provincial law.

If the credit bureau insists that it hasn't found sufficient evidence to warrant removing the erroneous information, ask them to note on your file that the information in question is "in dispute." Better yet, exercise your right to insert up to 100 words into your file. This is your chance to explain your side of the story—to present your version of the facts and tell potential creditors what really happened. Believe it or not, your statement will be taken seriously by credit grantors and could make the difference between a "yes" or a "no" the next time you apply for a loan.

How to tell when it's time to call it quits

Each year, more than 50,000 Canadian households file for bankruptcy—approximately one out of every two hundred households. For many, filing for bankruptcy is the wisest financial move they could make; for others, it's a poor decision that comes with an enormous price tag.

It's hard to think rationally about your bankruptcy options when you're fielding embarrassing phone calls from creditors while you're at home and at work. While you don't want to throw in the towel too easily, it's important to know how to tell when it's time to call it quits. As a rule of thumb, if your high-interest consumer debt (credit card bills, car loans, etc.) exceeds more than 25 percent of your income, bankruptcy is probably your best bet.

What to do before you throw in the towel

Of course, there's plenty you can do before you get to that point. If you're lucky and you spot the warning signs early enough, you may be able to head off bankruptcy altogether. Here are some steps you should take if you think you're headed for a financial meltdown:

- **Get in touch with your creditors.** Explain why you aren't able to make your payments right now and ask them if they'll either give you more time to repay your debts or reduce the amount of your monthly payments.

- **Go for credit counselling.** Have someone help you to take a realistic look at your financial situation and help you to determine whether you'd be better off declaring bankruptcy or working at paying off your debts. (Note: According to Eric Tyson and Tony Martin, authors of *Personal Finance for Dummies,* some of the credit card bureaus are funded by the credit card companies themselves—something that can lead them to provide less-than-objective advice. Debtor beware!)

- **Consider getting a debt consolidation loan.** Of course, it's only a good idea to go this route if you're able to obtain a loan that will bring down your monthly payments and reduce the amount of interest that you're paying, and if you have the self-discipline necessary to cut up your credit cards so that you won't fall into the same trap again.

- **Don't use the services of loan brokers.** There are less expensive ways to bring your debt problems under control.

- **Obtain a Consolidation Order.** If you live in British Columbia, Alberta, Saskatchewan, Nova Scotia, or Prince Edward Island, you can apply for a Consolidation Order, which allows you to repay your debts over a three-year period, frees you from both creditor harassment and wage garnishment, and allows you to hold on to your assets (something that you're not able to do if you declare bankruptcy). You simply make a series of debt payments to the court, which then distributes your payments to your creditors. Note: A similar plan known as Voluntary Deposit (a.k.a. the "Lacombe Law") is available in Quebec. It allows you to make a minimum payment to the courts as determined by your income and number of dependents.

Just a little bit bankrupt

While it's not possible to be "a little bit pregnant," it is possible to be "a little bit bankrupt." Instead of declaring full bankruptcy—when the bankruptcy trustee takes charge of your assets, sells them, and distributes the proceeds to your creditors—you may have the option of filing a consumer proposal instead.

A consumer proposal is basically a game plan for repaying all or a portion of your debts. It's an option for you (and/or you and your partner) if you have less than $75,000 of consumer debt, excluding your mortgage.

Show Me the Money!

It's possible to submit a consumer proposal or to file for full bankruptcy individually or as a couple. You and your partner will be permitted to take these steps together if your debts are substantially the same—something that simplifies the process and can save you money.

Here's how it works: a bankruptcy trustee (or someone appointed by the Superintendent of Bankruptcy) helps you to size up your assets, tally up your debts, and come up with a plan for paying your creditors. The bankruptcy trustee then files your proposal with the Official Trustee and subsequently submits a report expressing his or her opinion about whether the proposal appears to be fair and reasonable and whether he or she believes that you will be able to stick to it. Copies of your proposal and the bankruptcy trustee's report are then sent to your creditors.

Because you're generally asking them to forgive a portion of your debts, to lower your monthly payments, and/or to extend the period of time you have to repay the debt, your creditors are given up to 45 days to consider your proposal. They are asked to send a note to the bankruptcy trustee accepting or rejecting your proposal. Those who fail to respond are considered to have accepted your proposal.

If a sufficient number of your creditors turn down your proposal, they will be in a position to take legal steps to recover the money you owe them.

If a sufficient number of creditors accept the proposal, then it becomes legally binding on you and your creditors and you will all be expected to live up to the terms of the agreement. You'll be able to hold on to whatever goods you've accumulated over the years as long as you meet your obligations under the repayment plan. What's more, you'll prevent your unsecured creditors from being able to take legal steps to recover the money you owe them (examples: seizing property or garnisheeing your wage) as long as you meet your obligations. (Note: if you fail to live up to your end of the bargain, the proposal can be declared null and void.)

While writing a consumer proposal is a more pleasant alternative to filing for full bankruptcy, don't kid yourself: the process is anything but fun. You've narrowly escaped the need to declare full bankruptcy, but you've sentenced yourself to months or even years of penny-pinching as you attempt to fight your way back on to solid financial ground. In the end, however, assuming you meet your obligations, the bankruptcy trustee will issue a certificate of full performance and this particular chapter of your life will finally be behind you.

The pros and cons of declaring bankruptcy

The decision to declare bankruptcy is seldom an easy one to make, mainly because there's so much at stake. Here's a quick list of the pros and cons:

Pros

- Once you have declared bankruptcy, your unsecured creditors are no longer able to take legal steps to recover their debts from you (example: garnisheeing your wages).
- Certain types of debts can be erased entirely, including credit card bills, medical bills, car loan payments, utility bills, rent payments, tax bills, and student loans.
- In most provinces, you are allowed to keep certain property or assets: typically around $2,000 worth of furnishings and $1,000 worth of personal effects. You may also be permitted to keep a few thousand dollars worth of "tools of the trade" that you need in order to earn an income—your computer and your fax machine, for example.

- If you've spent months dealing with high-pressure phone calls and threatening letters from creditors, it can be a tremendous relief to know that the worst is behind you now.

Cons

- Some types of debts are not dischargeable. They remain on the books, like it or not. Child support, alimony, and court-ordered fines and penalties—including all those parking tickets you've ignored over the years!—don't disappear just because you've decided that it's time to wave a financial white flag.

- Anyone requesting a copy of your credit report during the next seven years will know that you filed for bankruptcy. This will make it difficult for you to obtain credit until your financial slate is wiped clean. (In some provinces, it will show up on your credit rating for as long as 14 years if you've previously declared bankruptcy.)

- Filing for bankruptcy costs money—and obviously that's the one thing you don't have! You can expect to fork over anywhere from a couple of hundred to a couple of thousand dollars to cover all the court filing charges and legal fees associated with declaring bankruptcy.

- Declaring bankruptcy can be humiliating. The process requires that you bare your financial soul to the court-appointed bankruptcy trustee, whose job is to see that your creditors recover as much of your property as possible. Unfortunately, while many people who declare bankruptcy experience feelings of shame and guilt, many are too embarrassed to talk about their feelings with family members and friends, because of the stigma involved in admitting that you have declared personal bankruptcy.

What to expect if you decide to declare bankruptcy

When you declare bankruptcy, your property is given to a bankruptcy trustee, who then sells it and distributes the money to your creditors. You are required to co-operate with him or her throughout the proceedings. Here are just a few of your responsibilities as set out in the Bankruptcy and Insolvency Act:

- You must be completely open with the bankruptcy trustee. You must declare all of your assets, including those assets that you disposed of during the past year or gave away during the previous five years. This involves handing over all of your financial records: insurance policies, tax records, bank and credit card statements, and more.

- You must surrender your credit cards so that the bankruptcy trustee can arrange to have them cancelled.

- You must meet with the official receiver at a designated place and time to discuss the bankruptcy proceedings and otherwise co-operate with the bankruptcy proceedings.

- You must ensure that the trustee receives copies of a statement of your financial affairs within five days of the bankruptcy, and you must examine these statements yourself to ensure that they are accurate.

- You will have to file two tax returns for the calendar year in which you became bankrupt: one for the period from January 1 until the date when you declared bankruptcy, and one from that point until December 31. The bankruptcy trustee may ask you to hand over all, or a portion of, any tax refund that you're entitled to so that it can be distributed to your creditors.

The penalties for noncompliance are rather stiff: anyone who is found to be in violation of the terms of the Bankruptcy and Insolvency Act can be fined as much as $10,000 and/or sentenced to up to three years in jail.

You can find out more about what is involved in declaring bankruptcy by visiting the Office of the Superintendent of Bankruptcy's Web site at **osb-bsf.ic.gc.ca** or by contacting one of the offices listed in Appendix B.

Three

WILL THAT BE ONE INCOME
OR TWO?

There's no doubt about it: the dual-income family is here to stay. For a variety of complex reasons—not the least of which is economics—the single-income family has found its way onto the endangered species list. More often than not, Canadian families are relying on two paycheques just to get by.

Money Talk

"A family with two incomes, a home, two cars, and a large mortgage can be shaken to the core by the loss of one of these two incomes."

Source: Judith Maxwell, "Family Security in Insecure Times," in the Vanier Institute of the Family, *From Kitchen Table to Boardroom Table.*

Consider the facts:

- Thirty years ago, only about one-third of couples were dual-income earners. A mere generation later, dual-income households have become the norm, with 70 percent of couples bringing home two paycheques.

- To earn the average household income of approximately $50,000, most Canadian families require two paycheques (see Table 3.1).

- In nearly half of dual-income households, the female partner brings in between one-quarter and one-half of the family's income (see Table 3.2).

Table 3.1: Percentage of Nonelderly Families with Two or More Earners by Level of Family Income, 1994

Annual family income	Percentage of families with two or more wage earners
$80,000 or more	93
$70,000 to 79,999	90
$60,000 to 69,999	86
$50,000 to 59,999	82
$40,000 to 49,999	73
$30,000 to 39,999	59
$20,000 to 29,999	45
Under $20,000	19

Source: Statistics Canada; Vanier Institute of the Family, *From Kitchen Table to Boardroom Table.*

Table 3.2: Wife's annual earnings as a percentage of couple's annual earnings

	1–24%	25–49%	50–74%	75–99%
All couples, both employed	30	46	19	5
All couples, both employed full-time, full-year	13	61	23	3
Couples with no children, both employed	23	47	23	6
Couples with no children, both employed full-time, full-year	11	59	26	4
Couples with children, both employed	33	46	17	4
Couples with children, both employed full-time, full-year	14	61	21	3

Source: Statistics Canada; Vanier Institute of the Family, *From Kitchen Table to Boardroom Table.*

- Single income households are much more likely to be living below the poverty line than dual-income households. The poverty rate among two-parent families with a single earner is 27 percent as compared to a poverty rate of just 7 percent when there are two wage earners in the family.
- Female parents are much more likely to stay at home to raise children than male parents (see Table 2.3).
- A growing number of women have become the chief breadwinners for their families. The percentage of dual-income households in which the female partner's earnings exceed those of the male partner increased from 11 percent in 1967 to 25 percent in 1993.

Table 3.3: Annual employment activity of husbands, wives, and single parents, 1994

Family members under 65 years of age	Full-time, full-year	Part-time or part-year	No employment
		%	
Husbands with children any age	75	18	7
Husbands with children under 7	75	19	6
Husbands with no children	63	21	16
Male single parent	55	21	24
Wives with no children	44	27	29
Wives with children any age	41	33	26
Wives with children under 7	36	36	28
Female single parents	32	25	43
Female single parents with children under 7	22	29	49

Note: "Full-time, full-year" means 49 or more weeks of full-time employment (30 or more hours each week). "Part-time and/or part-year" means working less than 30 hours per week and/or less than 49 weeks during the year (annual paid leave is counted as employment).

Source: Statistics Canada; Vanier Institute of the Family, *From Kitchen Table to Boardroom Table.*

The rest of the story

If the decision about whether to work outside the home or stay at home with your kids were merely a matter of finances, you'd have your answer in a flash. Key some numbers into your calculator, hit the total, and—voila!—your decision would be made for you.

Unfortunately, complex issues like these can rarely be boiled down to a simple financial calculation. There are so many other issues to consider, like how you feel about being a working or stay-at-home parent and what the long-term career costs are of dropping out of the workforce to raise a family.

Consider what the Vanier Institute of the Family says about the impact of the shift from single-income to dual-income households on Canadian families in its recent report *From the Kitchen Table to the Boardroom*: "The growth in the number of dual-income families has had an enormous impact on family life. It has brought into question the traditional roles of women and men, raised concern about the capacity of families to provide care for dependents, and, in many instances, has placed increasing demands on women, who continue to shoulder the majority of household and domestic labour. For many families, it has also raised issues of time management; co-ordinating schedules, and simply finding time to meet the demands of work while fulfilling family responsibilities."

Don't shoot the messenger

Before we get any further along in this chapter, allow me to insert a brief note about terminology. I personally hate the terms "working parent" and "stay-at-home parent," but I've yet to find any workable alternatives. I know that parents who are at home with their children are "working parents," too—and I know that they often do anything but "stay-at-home." They're too busy volunteering at their children's schools, taking their kids to the park to play, and sometimes even running part-time businesses on the side. So if you're tempted to throw a tomato at me because you don't like the fact that I call parents who work outside the home "working parents" and parents who work inside the home "stay-at-home parents," please think about throwing that tomato at the folks who write the dictionary. It's *their* fault I wasn't able to come up with the perfect term!

According to the U.S. National Center for Health Statistics, 80 percent of working women will become pregnant at some point during their working lives

This chapter of the book was one of the toughest ones for me to write, not just because of the terminology issue, but also because I discovered that there is no "right answer" that will apply to all families—even to families who have virtually identical financial situations, for Pete's sake!

I danced around the chapter for an entire week, trying to figure out how I was going to take a financial approach to an issue that, for many parents, often has very little to do with money. At one point I even tried to convince myself that the book didn't really need a chapter on this topic, but that was just the coward in me looking for an easy way to wriggle out of facing that blank computer screen day after day! In the end, I decided that there were two separate issues involved—the number crunching and the soul searching—and that I'd have to tackle them both if this chapter was going to have anything valuable to say.

Here goes!

The hidden costs of working

Let's start by tackling the easiest part of the working versus staying-at-home issue first—the dollars and cents part:

Money Talk

"We have always worked under the assumption that one of us would be staying home part-time. The definition of 'part-time' has changed over the years, but the importance hasn't. At this point, I'm not interested in pursuing a full-time career. I find that working three days per week is ideal."
- *Louise, 28, mother of one.*

If you worked through the budget exercises in the previous chapter, you've already got a good sense of your financial health (e.g., whether you're earning more than you spend, or vice versa). Now all you need to do is fiddle with a few of the lines in your budget to assess the financial fallout of staying at home versus working outside the home. Simply carry forward the numbers that you listed in Table 2.4 to Table 3.4 below and then start playing with some alternative scenarios—like what would happen if you went from two incomes to one (or even one-and-a-half).

Table 3.4: Income vs. Expenses

INCOME	DUAL-INCOME	SINGLE-INCOME
Your employment income	_____	_____
Your partner's employment income	_____	_____
Bonuses	_____	_____
Investment income	_____	_____
Rental income	_____	_____
Spousal support	_____	_____
Child support	_____	_____
Other sources of income	_____	_____
Total Income	_____	_____
EXPENSES	**DUAL-INCOME**	**SINGLE-INCOME**
Taxes and other income deductions		
Income tax	_____	_____
Canada/Quebec pension plan	_____	_____

continued...

EXPENSES	DUAL-INCOME	SINGLE-INCOME
Company pension plan contributions	_____	_____
Employment Insurance premiums	_____	_____
Union dues	_____	_____
Other deductions	_____	_____
Household expenses		
Rent or mortgage	_____	_____
Property taxes	_____	_____
House insurance	_____	_____
Utilities (heat, hydro, water)	_____	_____
Service contracts (cleaning, lawn care, snow removal, etc.)	_____	_____
Telephone	_____	_____
Cable TV	_____	_____
Household equipment	_____	_____
Household repair	_____	_____
Other	_____	_____
Food		
Groceries	_____	_____
Restaurant meals and takeout food	_____	_____
Other	_____	_____
Transportation		
Car loan payments	_____	_____
Gasoline	_____	_____
Maintenance/repairs	_____	_____
License fees (vehicle and driver's license)	_____	_____
Car insurance	_____	_____
Tolls and parking fees	_____	_____
Bus, subway, or commuter train fares	_____	_____
Taxis	_____	_____
Other	_____	_____
Personal care		
Clothing	_____	_____
Dry cleaning	_____	_____
Hair salon	_____	_____

continued...

EXPENSES	DUAL-INCOME	SINGLE-INCOME
Health club membership	_____	_____
Other	_____	_____
Debt repayment		
Credit cards	_____	_____
Line of credit	_____	_____
Student loans	_____	_____
Other debts	_____	_____
Entertainment		
Movies	_____	_____
Concerts	_____	_____
Vacations	_____	_____
Gifts	_____	_____
Books	_____	_____
Video rentals	_____	_____
Hobbies	_____	_____
Wine, beer, and other alcoholic beverages	_____	_____
Other	_____	_____
Professional services		
Accountant	_____	_____
Lawyer	_____	_____
Financial advisor	_____	_____
Health care		
Drugs	_____	_____
Dental care	_____	_____
Eye care	_____	_____
Other	_____	_____
Educational expenses		
Tuition	_____	_____
Books	_____	_____
Other	_____	_____
Insurance		
Life insurance	_____	_____
Disability insurance	_____	_____
Medical insurance	_____	_____

continued…

INCOME	DUAL-INCOME	SINGLE-INCOME
Other expenses		
Child care	_____	_____
Charitable donations	_____	_____
Other	_____	_____
Total Expenses	_____	_____

You'll want to pay particular attention to the lines of your budget that are most likely to be affected by your decision to work or stay at home. They include:

1. **Income.** If you or your partner decide to leave your job, you can expect this figure to drop significantly—unless, of course, you're intending to make other changes to offset the income loss. The breadwinner, for example, might decide to look for a better-paying job, or the stay-at-home parent might decide to try to bring in some extra income by running a business from home. Note: Don't forget to factor in the value of any benefits you or your partner receive through your employers. A dental plan is pure gold to a family with young children!

2. **Child care.** According to the latest figures from the Centre for International Statistics at the Canadian Council on Social Development, in 1998 Canadian parents paid approximately $6,000 for full-time child care for an infant and $5,000 for full-time child care for a toddler or preschooler. You don't have to do much number crunching to see how much money you would save on this line of your budget by staying home as opposed to paying for full-time childcare for two or more children.

In 1994-95, 40 percent of Canadian children under five were cared for by people other than their own parents for an average of 27 hours per week: 56 percent in someone else's home, 22 percent in their own home, 20 percent in child-care centres, and 2 percent in other types of arrangements.

Source: Statistics Canada; Vanier Institute of the Family, *From Kitchen Table to Boardroom Table.*

3. **Transportation.** The cost savings on the transportation budget line is a lot less clear-cut. Some single-income families consider the second car to be sacred—the only thing that keeps the stay-at-home parent sane. Others view it as an unnecessary frill. Only you can decide how important it is to you to have a second car. If you're lucky enough to live on a bus route or to live across the street from a recreation centre, a park, and a shopping mall, you might decide that you don't need that second vehicle after all. (You'll find out about the true cost of running a car in Chapter 6.)

4. **Food.** While your family still needs to eat whether you work outside the home or stay at home, you may find that the amount of money you spend on groceries and both takeout and restaurant meals changes significantly if you make the switch from being a dual-income to a single-income family and there's one parent at home to prepare meals. (Note: Part of the adjustment to this part of your budget is due to sheer necessity, of course: there aren't the same funds available to pick up a pizza every time you're feeling too tired to cook.)

5. **Clothing.** If you wear your "street clothes" to work each day, you're not going to see a huge difference in this budget category if you decide to leave your job. If, on the other hand, you are expected to wear suits or dressy clothing to work, you may find yourself spending a significant amount of money on clothing, dry-cleaning bills, and so on. If you left your job, or started working from home as a freelance consultant, you would dramatically reduce your expenditures in this area.

6. **Miscellaneous.** Ah, miscellaneous. That mysterious black hole in your budget. You may find that the miscellaneous category goes on a drastic reducing diet if you become a single-income family—again, partially due to necessity, but also because there are fewer places to spend your money. You'll no longer be expected to pitch in $10 to buy a gift for a co-worker who just had a baby or to buy $20-worth of Girl Guide cookies from your boss's daughter. These "little things" can really add up, often to $500 or more per year for someone working outside of the home.

As you can see, there are a lot of hidden costs to working. You spend more money on transportation, childcare, clothing, and perhaps other types of items, than you would if only one of you were working. These costs can really sneak up on you, so sometimes it can be a bit of a shock to tally them up and consider the bottom line. Some couples who do this calculation find that they're not taking home much more money with both of them working than they would if just one of them were working. Others find that they're actually further ahead financially if they lose the second paycheque.

The hidden costs of staying at home

While most parents find it relatively easy to assess the short-term costs of staying at home to raise a family, what many fail to consider are the long-term financial implications of that choice.

First of all, there's the fact that you'll likely lose ground when it comes to saving for your retirement. When you're at home full-time with your children, you don't have any employment earnings, so you can't make registered retirement savings plan (RRSP) contributions in your own name (unless, of course, you've got some unused contribution room left from previous years). While your partner can use up some of his or her RRSP contributions by starting up a spousal plan in your name, you'll simply end up dividing up the pot of money that your partner might otherwise have contributed to his or her own RRSP, which will result in a lower standard of living for your family come retirement time than you would enjoy if you'd both been working full-time and maxing out your RRSP contributions. (Of course, if one of your children grows up to be the next great NHL superstar and decides to provide for you in your old age, you'll be ahead of the game financially. Just be forewarned that it doesn't always work out that way!)

Money Talk

"Women pay a heavier financial and sometimes professional price as childbearers of the species. For some reason, our society doesn't recognize the fact that raising the next generation of Canadians is work. As a result, those who leave the paid labour force periodically or permanently face lost income now and lower retirement savings later."

Source: Financial planning expert Joanne Thomas Yaccato, *Chatelaine*.

Second, there are the career costs associated with deciding to drop out of the workforce for an extended period of time. You're likely to miss out on promotions and you may quickly lose touch with developments in your industry or profession, something that could necessitate a period of retraining when you decide to go back to work again.

Third, the stay-at-home partner loses his or her financial safety net. If your marriage breaks up or the breadwinner dies suddenly, the stay-at-home partner could find himself or herself thrown back into the workforce with few, if any, marketable skills.

the Bottom line

The grass isn't necessarily greener on the stay-at-home side of the fence. A recent U.S. study concluded that two-income families are generally happier and healthier than families in which only the male partner works. They have fewer financial worries and both partners are less likely to suffer from depression than parents who are at home full-time raising their children. "The news about the two-career couple today is very good indeed," write Rosalind C. Barnett and Caryl Rivers, authors of *She Works/He Works: How Two-Income Families are Happier, Healthier, and Better-Off*, a book based on the study.

That's why it's important to look at more than just the bottom line when you're making this all-important decision. There are times when it makes sense to continue as a two-paycheque family, even if your childcare costs and other work-related expenses end up wiping out the second income altogether. If, for example, you're in a profession where it's difficult to take a couple of years off (if you're self-employed, the vice-president of a large corporation, or a doctor with a busy medical practice, for example), you might decide that it's worthwhile to continue working outside the home, even if you're not making any money over the short-run. After all, you'll be forking over major amounts of cash for childcare-related expenses for only a couple of years.

What the numbers won't tell you

Up until now, however, we've been focussing on the dollars-and-cents component of the working versus staying at home issue. What we haven't tackled yet are all of the nonmonetary aspects of this decision, such as how you might feel about leaving the workforce to be at home with your children.

Facts and Figures

According to a recent Statistics Canada report, while 73 percent of Canadian women and 68 percent of Canadian men believe that women should contribute to family income, 51 percent of women and 59 percent of men believe that both parents working outside the home is harmful to preschoolers.

Source: *Maclean's*.

If you're someone who gets a great deal of satisfaction from working, and who thinks she'd be completely stir-crazy by the end of her first day as a stay-at-home mom, then it probably makes more sense for you to keep your job, even if you can afford to stay home. (Think about it: how much quality time are you going to manage to spend with your kids if you feel bored or depressed all the time?)

The flip side of the coin also applies, of course. If being at home with your children is extremely important to you, you may decide that you're going to stay home with them, whether you and your partner can actually afford to lose that second income or not. That's what Cindy, a 40-year-old mother of two, and her partner, John, decided to do. They've never looked back. "We suffered financially when I quit my full-time job, but I wouldn't change a thing," she explains. "It has given us both a remarkable number of memories with our children that we would have missed if we both kept working in Toronto and commuting."

Making a decision you can live with

Whether you decide to stay at home with your children or continue working, what's important is how comfortable you and your partner feel about the decision that you have made. That's why the two of you should make this decision together.

Some couples find that there's no decision to be made. They've always known what's right for them. This was certainly the case for Fiona, a 32-year-old mother of six, and her husband Christopher. "My husband's mother stayed home full-time until he was 18 years old, so he grew up thinking that's what other moms did. We always knew that when there were kids, I would stay home with them, and he would go to work."

David, 38, and Phyllis, 37, parents of two young children, also found it relatively easy to make their decision. In their case, they decided that it made the most sense for them both to continue working. "We looked both at financials and at the impact on Phyllis' career if she were to stop working,"

David recalls. "She had recently completed her master's degree and was really just getting started with new responsibilities. We felt that having her return to work was the best decision for our family, provided we could get quality daycare. "

Money Talk

"We were both commuting to work, so the cost of childcare would have been astronomical. We didn't decide that I would stay home until after the baby was born. I never realized the extent of a mother's love until then. I couldn't bear the thought of leaving her every day. We decided then that I was staying home even if we had to start selling furniture."
- *Melinda, 33, mother of three.*

Kristin and her husband Jeff, both 30, reached a similar conclusion. "We briefly discussed the issue of one of us staying home, but it was not feasible," she explains. "I am the primary breadwinner in our family and my husband was not interested in staying home. Before returning to work, I did a quick calculation of how much money we would need to meet all of our current financial obligations—no frills, just the basics. With just Jeff's salary, there was a shortfall, so I figured out how many other children I would need to look after to make enough money. It turns out I would need to look after four children in addition to my son Nathan to make staying at home work. I wasn't willing to do that because I didn't feel Nathan would be getting much benefit from my being at home if I had four other children to care for."

Other couples find that the decision is a lot less clear cut. They have to do a lot of number crunching and soul-searching before they are able to decide what's best for their family. Kate, a 40-year-old mother of two, and her husband David spent a lot of time trying to figure out how they could go from living on two incomes to one after their first child arrived: "We were quite committed to having one of us at home with the children. We worked over our budget many times in advance in order to ensure that we would know what our budget ceiling would be for such things as vehicle, rent, and so on." In the end, they found a way to trim their budget enough to meet their goal of having Kate stay at home with their children.

How can you quit when you're the boss?

In most cases, the idea of dropping out of the workforce—even temporarily—is nothing more than pie in the sky if you happen to be self-employed. As much as your clients may try to tell you that they'll be banging on your door when you hang out your shingle again in five years' time, the odds of this actually happening are slim to none. The business that you worked so hard to build over a period of time can be reduced to nothing overnight if you have to start handing your valued customers over to your competitors.

A better option for self-employed workers who are eager to be at home with their children is to look for ways to scale down the business or to reduce their involvement in it for a certain period of time. Some entrepreneurs will cut back on the number of hours they devote to the business each week. Others will hire someone to run the business so they can take some time off. Both of these solutions allow the entrepreneurial parent to buy some time away from work without folding the business entirely.

Trimming your budget

If you decide that you or your partner will be staying home after Junior arrives, you'll need to go back through your budget line by line and look for areas in which you can boost your income or slash your expenses. (If you flip back to Table 3.4, you'll have all the numbers you need at your fingertips.)

Here are the major areas that are worth zeroing in on:

Income

1. Look for ways to boost your income without increasing your work-related expenses. The breadwinner might negotiate for a raise or start looking for a better-paying job, or the parent who's at home with the children might try to find a part-time job or start a home-based business in order to bring in a little extra income. (Note: Despite what you might assume by watching the Bill Gateses of the world in action, being self-employed is anything but a get-rich-quick scheme. Studies have shown that it takes from one to three years for a "typical" small business to start turning a profit.)

the Bottom line

"The decision about my staying home was pretty much made for us when the job I was doing ended. I did go to work supply teaching for a couple of years, but the stress and the aggravation was not worth it for the money I was making. Since my husband has a very good job, it was easy for us to decide that I would quit working

and stay at home. As for being feasible or not, we decided to make it feasible: we decided to continue to be a one-car family, to remain in a smaller house, and so on. And we haven't regretted our decision."
- *Leigh, 31, mother of two.*

Household expenses

2. Reduce your rent payments by moving to a smaller apartment or house, or by relocating to a less expensive area.

3. Reduce your mortgage payments by moving to a less expensive area, buying a smaller house, or increasing the amortization period (the length of time it takes to pay off your mortgage) the next time your mortgage comes up for renewal. (Note: While the whole idea of extending the amortization period on your mortgage contradicts everything you ever learned about borrowing money, there are times when such a move is justified. If taking a longer amortization period makes it possible for you to stay at home with your children and that's important to you, you should consider the additional interest costs that you'll incur as part of the cost of staying at home with your kids.)

4. Obtain quotes from other house insurance companies to ensure that you're getting the best possible value for your insurance dollar. If you find that you're paying too much for insurance, switch to a more cost-effective policy.

5. Save money on your utility bills by insulating your home better, replacing any ancient appliances that gobble up energy (e.g., freezers), switching from an electric water heater to a gas water heater, and/or by looking for ways to conserve energy around the house (e.g., turning the thermostat down a degree or two, hanging your wet clothes on the clothesline rather than popping them into the dryer, and so on).

Show Me the Money!

Some hydroelectric utilities are willing to come to your home to suggest ways that you could reduce your energy consumption. In some communities, this type of energy audit is free; in others, you'll have to pay a nominal fee. Either way, the energy audit could put a whole lot of money back in your pocket.

6. Cancel as many service contracts as possible (cleaning, lawn care, snow removal, etc.), get rid of a lot of those gimmicky phone features that cost

a couple of dollars apiece, cancel your cable TV altogether or cut back to a no-frills cable TV package, and look for other ways to save money on your household expenses.

7. Make sure that you're signed up for the long distance savings package that's best suited to your family. Some are ideal for people who do a lot of phoning during primetime; others are best for people who do all of their calling in the evening and on the weekend. The best way to find out which one would be best for your family is to ask various phone company representatives to recalculate your last phone bill based on their particular long distance savings plan. (Hey, if they want your business, they should be prepared to do a little work to earn it!)

8. Come up with creative ways to negotiate for the best possible deals on home repairs. If your roof needs replacing, chances are the other houses on your street that were built at the same time need replacing, too. Get together with your neighbours and approach area roofing companies to see if they'll give you a group discount on roof repairs.

9. Buy your furniture from wholesalers and through discount outlets. If you're shopping at a regular retail outlet, be sure to check the scratch and dent room to see if there are any pieces of furniture worth buying. Your furniture is going to take a bit of a beating from dinky cars and hockey sticks anyway; you might as well save some money and buy it pre-scratched!

10. Decorate with paint rather than wallpaper, and look for seconds and ends of rolls when you're shopping for carpet or flooring.

Automotive expenses

11. If you're not a good negotiator, hire an auto negotiator to do your dirty work for you. According to a recent article in *Chatelaine,* you can expect to pay about $250 for the services of an auto negotiator, but you could save yourself far more than that by getting a better-than-average deal on the vehicle.

12. If you don't need a car on a day-to-day basis because you have access to an excellent public transit system, consider joining a car co-op or car-sharing group. You will have access to a pool of cars that you can book as the need arises (e.g., when you do your weekly grocery shopping or if you are headed out of town).

Money Talk

"Make saving a game. Trick yourself by putting away everything you save with coupons. Or throw all your change in a jar. Then use that money to have some fun you didn't think you could afford."

Source: Melodie Moore, publisher of The Skinflint News, in Good Housekeeping.

Food

13. Consider joining—or starting—a food-buying co-op so that you can purchase food directly from wholesalers, something that can cut your food-buying costs by 25 percent or more.

14. Don't go to the same grocery store from week to week. Compare prices by checking out the various grocery store flyers each week and then give that week's business to the store that is offering the best prices on the items you need.

15. Don't step foot in a grocery store without a grocery list. It's the impulse buys, not the basic grocery items, that really add to your weekly grocery bill.

16. Know your prices. Just because an item is "on sale" doesn't necessarily mean it's a good buy. Nor are generics always cheaper than name brands.

17. Don't forget to check out the top and bottom shelves when you're looking for a particular item: the most expensive items are deliberately placed at eye level, where they're easier to find.

18. Don't just wander aimlessly in the grocery store, buying whatever catches your eye. Plan your grocery list ahead of time so that you'll have the ingredients you need on hand to make healthy, low-cost dinners from scratch. (If you don't take the time to do this, you'll simply end up ordering pizza because you don't have enough ingredients on hand to make anything!)

19. Think big. You can usually save about 25 cents per pound on meat by opting for the family-sized packages. Either use the entire package at one time to make a large batch of casseroles or divide the package into smaller portions that can be popped into the freezer for use at another time. Don't make the same mistake with perishable items, however: there's nothing more discouraging than watching a fridge-full of lettuce turn brown because you couldn't get through it all in time.

20. Check your cash register tape before you drive out of the parking lot. One moneysaving expert swears that one in ten grocery items are improperly keyed in—something that could end up costing you a small fortune.

21. Make your meals from scratch. It's far less expensive to make your own tuna casserole than to buy one out of the freezer at the grocery store. It's also a whole lot tastier! If you hate spending hours in the kitchen by yourself, consider starting a co-operative kitchen. (A co-operative kitchen involves pulling a group of people together and spending an afternoon or an evening cooking in bulk. Everyone pools their money to buy ingredients, pitches in with the preparation, and then takes home a bunch of homemade entrées that they can store in their freezer.)

22. Find creative alternatives to frozen dinners. According to a recent article in *Chatelaine,* it's sometimes possible to buy frozen dinners from airline food suppliers for just half of what you would expect to pay for a supermarket frozen dinner.

23. Instead of buying baby food in jars, make your own. Simply purée mashed fruits or vegetables, adding small amounts of water until the baby food has reached the desired consistency. There's an added bonus to going this route: your baby will become accustomed to the types of food that your family eats on a regular basis before he actually starts eating table food!

24. Grow your own vegetables so that you won't spend as much money on produce during the summer months. If you're not much of a gardener, make weekly visits to the local farmers' market or purchase a share in an organic farm. (We purchased a share in a local organic farm a few years ago and had delicious fresh produce show up on our doorstep on a weekly basis. There was far more produce than our family could reasonably eat, so we shared our basket full of goodies with our neighbours. Over the course of the growing season, we managed to save a couple of hundred dollars over what we would have paid for the same types of produce in a grocery store.)

25. Don't get hypnotized by the large warehouse stores. Bigger isn't necessarily better. In fact, you could find yourself paying more for certain types of items than you would at a regular grocery store. You really have to know your prices.

Money Talk

"We order out maybe once a year and never eat in restaurants. We prefer to make meals ahead in bulk and freeze them for those nights when we have no desire to cook. We enjoy backyard picnics in the summer and living room picnics in the winter."
- *Fiona, 32, mother of six.*

Dining out

26. Figure out how often you can afford to eat out and how much you can afford to spend. You may find that you can afford one $30 dinner out a month—a nice break for the parent who's at home all day with the kids—or you may find that dinners out are one luxury you'll have to do without for at least the foreseeable future. If this is the case, you might want to consider doing some budget-friendly entertaining in your own home: swap invitations with another family with young children so that you can each enjoy occasional dinners out.

27. Find out if there's a special discount night at your favourite restaurant. Some restaurants, for example, let kids eat for free on Friday night.

Transportation

28. Car-pool to work or take public transit so that you can sell the second car and still leave the stay-at-home parent with a set of wheels at least some of the time.

29. Swap the gas-guzzler for a more fuel-efficient vehicle.

30. Consider sharing a car with another family. (Just make sure you resolve the insurance and maintenance issues up front.)

Personal care

31. Unless you're a regular at the gym, consider switching from an annual membership to a pay-as-you-go membership. If your health club doesn't offer this option—and, frankly, some of the big health club chains don't—call your local YMCA/YWCA instead.

Clothing

32. Shop at second-hand clothing stores as much as possible when you're buying clothes for both yourself and your children. You can pick up nearly-new clothing at a fraction of what you would pay for them new.

(If you've got expensive taste in clothing, don't despair: there are even consignment shops that specialize in gently used designer clothing!)

Money Talk

When you're hitting the second-hand shops, don't forget to bring along some of your own used clothing to sell. While you won't get a huge amount of money for each item, what you do get will help to make any items you purchase that much more affordable.

33. Learn to sew. You can save a tremendous amount of money on clothing—particularly children's clothing—if you sew even a portion of your wardrobe. (Note: If the mere word "sew" causes you to have horrible flashbacks about your grade eight home economics class, perhaps it would be best to skip this tip entirely. If, however, you were one of those home economics whiz kids who knew intuitively how to set a sleeve in an armhole, it's time to put those long-dormant talents to good use.)

34. Don't purchase any item that needs to be dry cleaned. Those $10 dry cleaning charges will quickly add up to more than what you paid for the item. The only exceptions to this hard and fast rule are business clothing and outer wear.

35. If you're purchasing new clothing for your children, try to shop at stores that will replace the item if it wears out before your child outgrows it. (This can save you a lot of money if you have an eight-year-old boy who's addicted to road hockey!)

36. Don't just fixate on the price tag. Keep in mind that an expensive pair of overalls that lasts through three kids may be cheaper in the long-run than a poor-quality pair that doesn't even make it through one kid.

37. Join any customer loyalty programs offered by your favourite retail clothing stores. You'll receive coupons and advance notice of sales.

38. Watch for end-of-season sales on name-brand merchandise. If you're a Land's End addict like I am, you might want to pay particular attention to the overstocks page on their Web site. The prices that are "On The Counter" are marked down more and more each day until they're sold out. Check it out for yourself by visiting the site at **www.landsend.com.**

39. Shop for seconds at manufacturers' retail outlets. Often the flaw is either unnoticeable or something you can repair yourself with a needle and thread.

40. Invite a group of women friends over for a clothing swap. Ask everyone to bring a half-dozen items of clothing that are in mint condition, but that they are no longer wearing. Take turns choosing from the pile of clothing and—voila!—you'll each have the makings of a new wardrobe and space for it in your clothes closet to boot.

Bank charges

41. Make sure that the type of bank account you're using is the one that best fits your family's needs. As Table 3.5 indicates, you may need to shop around to get the best possible deal. The Canadian Banker's Association suggests that you analyze your banking patterns (e.g., the number of deposits and withdrawals you make each month, whether you prefer in-branch or electronic banking, whether you need to have your cheques returned, and so on) and then try to find the account that will best meet your needs. Industry Canada has a nifty online tool that will do a lot of the legwork for you. The Financial Service Charges Calculator available online at **strategis.ic.gc.ca/SSG/ca01012e.html** allows you to compare the monthly service charges that you're currently paying with what you would pay if you were to move your banking to another financial institution.

42. Think your bank charges are excessive? Tell your bank manager to waive your service charges or you'll take your business elsewhere. Financial institutions hate to lose chequing account business because once people move their chequing accounts, they tend to move their mortgages, car loans, RRSPs, and other types of business, too.

Table 3.5: Average monthly bank charges, 1997–98

	9 in-branch banking transactions		35 electronic banking transactions	
	1997	1998	1997	1998
Bank of Montreal	$ 9.50	$ 9.50	$ 9.50	$11.50
Canada Trust	8.95	9.45	12.95	12.95
CIBC	10.00	10.00	11.80	11.80
Desjardins	11.55	11.95	12.10	10.30
Laurentian Bank	10.95	10.95	6.15	6.15
mbanx	13.00	13.00	13.00	13.00
Metro Credit Union	6.00	6.00	12.40	12.40
National Bank	8.75	15.00	14.28	10.35
National Trust	9.50	9.50	8.80	8.80
	1997	1998	1997	1998
Royal Bank	9.20	9.20	12.35	12.00
	1997	1998	1997	1998
Scotiabank	7.75	9.95	14.90	10.00
TD Bank	11.60	11.60	5.00	5.00

Source: Industry Canada data, *The Globe and Mail.*

43. When you're shopping around for a chequing account, be sure to consider such factors as
   - your preferred method of payment (e.g., cheque, credit card, debit card, telephone banking, Internet banking, or cash)
   - what fees are charged on this type of account and whether or not you will receive a rebate for the fee if you keep your account balance at or above a certain level)
   - the average monthly balance in your chequing account
   - how much this balance fluctuates over the course of a month
   - whether you need to have your cheques returned for either tax or record-keeping reasons.

When you're shopping around for a savings account, be sure to consider such factors as

- what maintenance fees you will be charged and whether or not there is an additional fee if your account balance drops below a certain amount
- whether you're allowed to write cheques on this account and, if so, what the fee is for writing a cheque
- the rate of interest you will be paid on your savings (both before and after compounding)
- whether or not interest rates are tiered (e.g., does the interest rate go up once your balance reaches a certain level?)

Credit and debt

44. Pay off any debts that you are carrying, starting with the debts with the highest interest rates. If you're carrying around department store credit card balances and other high-interest debt, get a lower-interest consolidation loan from your financial institution and then retire your department store credit card permanently.

45. Make sure that you're getting the best possible deal from your credit card company. Look for a card that offers a low (or no) annual fee, a low interest rate, and that rewards you for your business. For example, the TD GM Green VISA card allows you to earn credit towards the purchase of a GM-manufactured vehicle and Royal Bank's Canadian Plus VISA Gold allows you to earn air miles for each dollar charged on your card.

Facts and Figures

"Since American Airlines introduced the first frequent-flyer plan in 1981, membership in such programs has mushroomed to an estimated 75 million people worldwide. In Canada, roughly 60 percent of adults belong to at least one frequent-flyer plan—one of the highest participation rates in the world."

Source: John Schofield, "Sky High Bonanza," *Maclean's Guide to Personal Finance 1999.*

Entertainment

46. Rethink your definition of entertainment. It doesn't have to be expensive to be fun. Take your kids to a performance of a local amateur theatre troupe or take up a low-cost hobby as a family, such as hiking.

47. Take out a family membership if you're lucky to live near a major attraction such as the Vancouver Aquarium, the Royal Ontario Museum in Toronto, and Science North in Sudbury. Your membership will typically pay for itself after two or three visits.

48. Rent videos instead of going to the movies. (Hey, you'll be a couple of bucks ahead in the popcorn department alone!)

the Bottom line

"I took my kids to an amusement park and someone got sick. I had a headache, we spent fifty dollars, and hated the whole experience. That's the kind of spending I dislike. A lot of people don't question whether they're getting real pleasure for their money."

– Amy Dacyczyn, publisher of *The Tightwad Gazette,* in *Good Housekeeping.*

49. Trade in your old CDs for new ones at your nearest second-hand music store.

50. If you purchase a big-ticket item like a TV set or a VCR, watch the paper for the next few weeks. If you see the item you bought advertised for less money, take a copy of the advertisement back to the store and ask the store to give you the difference. In many cases, they will.

51. Purchase electronic games and other pricey electronic gizmos at your local consignment store. Then split the cost with another family and share it back and forth. (You'll not only save money: you'll also make it more difficult for your children to develop an electronic games addiction!)

52. Buy your sports equipment second-hand and sell all the unused sports equipment that you've accumulated in a corner of your garage at the same time.

53. Hit the library rather than the bookstore or the magazine stand.

54. Make your own wine and beer, either at home or at a commercial "u-brew" operation.

Money Talk

"When it comes to entertainment, we look for anything free. We make lots of visits to the local library and park and take advantage of recreation programs run by the city. We spend a lot of time with our kids doing things together that cost little money."
- *Leigh, 31, mother of two.*

Travel

55. Plan to travel out of season. You can expect to save 25 to 50 percent by timing your vacation properly. What's more, you'll beat the crowds. (Note: While this is easiest to accomplish before your children start school, you can probably get away with pulling your kids out of school for the odd family trip. Check with your child's teacher before you make your holiday plans so that you won't accidentally hit a week when there's something particularly special going on at school.)

56. Don't assume that you have to hop on a plane to "get away from it all." Sometimes the best vacation destinations can be found in your own backyard.

57. Go camping instead of staying in a hotel. You'll spend $25 a night as opposed to $75 or more.

58. If you're travelling with kids, stock your car with drinks and snacks before you leave home. That way, you can hit the highway rest stops for bathroom breaks without being forced to pay exorbitant prices for junk food.

59. Try to choose a hotel that allows kids to stay for free. Some of the major hotel chains don't charge for kids' meals eaten in the hotel dining room. Failing that, plan to have breakfast and possibly even lunch in your hotel room to save a bit of money.

60. If you're travelling by air, you'll get the lowest possible rate if you schedule your trip so that you leave on a Saturday, Tuesday, or Wednesday, and are away over a Saturday; and if you book your flight at least three weeks in advance.

61. If you're not in any hurry to get home, volunteer to be bumped if the airline flight is oversold. At a minimum, you'll pick up a voucher for $200 per person, perhaps considerably higher if the airline is particularly eager to get people to volunteer to wait until the next available flight.

Health care

62. If your family isn't covered by a drug plan and your family doctor prescribes an expensive drug, ask him or her if there's a less expensive generic drug that would do the trick.

63. If your family isn't covered by a dental plan, let your dentist know. Some dentists will reduce their fees for families who are on tight budgets.

64. If you live in a community with a dental school, make your appointments there instead. You will pay one-third to one-half of the going rate, and you'll be helping the next generation of dentists to learn the ropes.

Educational expenses

65. If you or your partner are attending college or university on a full-time or part-time basis, find out if there are bursaries or scholarships available to help offset the costs of tuition. Start by contacting the financial aid office at your school, but also be sure to check with your employer (or your partner's employer) to see if the company will pick up part or all of the cost of your educational expenses.

66. Purchase as many textbooks as possible second-hand. If the campus bookstore doesn't sell second-hand books, advertise on bulletin boards or place a small advertisement in the student newspaper. You might also want to check out the growing number of online bookstores that specialize in selling second-hand college and university textbooks.

Money Talk

"Each family's spending habits vary so widely, depending on factors from the type of child care they use to the kind of lifestyle that they lead, that it's almost impossible to generalize about how lucrative a second income actually is."
Source: Barbara Hetzer, *How Can I Ever Afford Children?*

Insurance

67. Don't buy more insurance than you need, but make sure that you buy enough. A good insurance broker will be able to help you to calculate the amount of insurance coverage you need—no more, no less.

68. Obtain quotes from more than one company so that you can be sure that you're getting the best possible value for your insurance dollar.

69. Consider giving all of your insurance business to one company if they're willing to give you a break on the overall cost.

Child care expenses

70. Send your child to a co-operative nursery school. Because parents play an active role in running the school, the per-hour rate for child care is considerably less.

71. Reduce the number of hours of child care you require. If one parent decides to stay at home full-time, there can be significant savings—typically $5,000 to $6,000 per year for each child requiring full-time care.

72. If you have more than one child, consider hiring an in-home caregiver rather than sending two or more children to an out-of-home child-care facility. It's often less expensive than paying for out-of-home child care spaces for each of your children, and it's certainly a lot more convenient to have someone come into your home than to have to shuttle your children to a family day care or child care centre when you're on your way to work.

Charitable donations

73. Consider contributing to your favourite charity in nonmonetary ways if you find yourself on a tight budget. Volunteers are in chronically short supply, so your offer to help with the next fundraising drive will no doubt be welcome.

In general

74. Consider bartering goods and services with others in your community. If you're a great cook, offer to swap bottles of your famous chili sauce for help weeding your perennial garden. Note: If there's a bartering system (e.g., a local economic trading system, or L.E.T.S. exchange) in your community, consider joining it. You'll have a far greater number of people to trade with than just those in your immediate circle of friends.

75. Take advantage of annual sales on particular types of goods. There's no better time to stock up on school supplies than in late August or early September, for example.

the Bottom line

"This was not a financial decision at all for us. We both felt we needed to work for the mental stimulation."
- Jackie, 31, mother of two.

As you can see, there are plenty of steps you can take to reduce the amount of income you require keep your family in the black. You'll also find plenty of other ideas elsewhere in this book.

Us, Inc.

Some couples decide that the ideal solution to the working-versus-staying-at-home dilemma is to have one or both parents start a small business. While this is a great idea in theory, the fact remains that not all small businesses turn a profit, and even those that do can take months—even years—to start breaking even.

If you're seriously thinking of launching a small business as a means of supplementing your family's income, it's important to do your homework first and to make sure that there's actually a market for the product or service you're intending to offer. After all, there's no point in spending a small fortune on lawn-care tools if there's a glut of gardening businesses in your community and you don't have a hope of competing with some of the more established firms.

Once you've determined that there is, in fact, a market for your product or service, you need to write a detailed financial plan for your business. You need to project your revenues and take into account every conceivable expense in order to determine when, if ever, your business will start turning a profit. When you're drafting your plan, it's important to factor in the hidden costs of running a business—things like inventory, equipment, phone bills, and so on. After all, that $20,000 in revenue you're projecting for your first year could disappear in the blink of an eye if you have to buy $10,000 worth of computer equipment and $10,000 worth of inventory to get your business up and running.

After you've looked long and hard at the finances, you need to stop and consider the time and commitment required to make your business successful. You don't want to discover after the fact that the business you launched so that you could stay at home with your kids is requiring 60 hours a week from you! Unfortunately, unless you've experienced entrepreneurship for yourself, it can be all too easy to underestimate the amount of sweat equity that goes into growing a business. So if you're a novice at this whole self-employment thing, you should definitely talk to other entrepreneurs with similar types of operations to find out how many hours they're putting in each week and use that as a rule of thumb.

You also need to know that your partner is 100 percent behind your decision to launch your own business—especially if some initial scrimping and saving is going to be required while you pull together the funds to launch and grow your business. Jim, a 37-year-old father of three, gives his spouse, Susan, full credit for doing without "frills" like a clothes dryer and bags of soil for their garden when they were trying to get the business up and running. "Sue has had a tremendous impact on the success of the business. She has made some huge sacrifices to get this thing going," he admits.

Money Talk

"Ken has worked to 'flatten' out our expenses by running credit balances with a lot of the monthly bills—hydro, water, cable, mortgage, and so on. We're usually paid ahead two or three months so that if he has a lean month in the business, the basics will be covered."
- Nicole, 28, mother of one.

It's scary enough to enter the ranks of the self-employed knowing full-well that you can always fall back on your partner's paycheque. If, however, you both decide to leave your jobs elsewhere to start a business together, it can be downright hair-raising. If you decide to go this route, you should take steps to create a financial safety net for your family. If you don't give some thought to these issues up front, you could find yourselves facing financial disaster if the business goes through a rough period, you're sued by a disgruntled customer, or you or your partner is permanently or temporarily disabled or—heaven forbid—killed in a car accident. This means setting up your business in a manner that will ensure that your personal assets are sheltered, carrying appropriate amounts of life insurance and disability insurance, and getting into the habit of setting aside some money each week so that you'll have enough funds stashed away to buy an umbrella on the next rainy day.

The moral of the story? Self-employment is not for the faint of heart. Make sure you take the plunge with both eyes wide open.

Four

The Wish List

Step right up, folks. It's time for a fast-paced game of paycheque roulette. Just give the old roulette wheel a spin, keep your eyes on the little red ball, and find out where this week's paycheque is going to go. It's spinning, spinning, spinning—and it's stopped. The ball has stopped on "car loan." Looks like you'll get to keep that minivan on the road for another week or two.

Do you sometimes feel like you're playing paycheque roulette—that there are far more demands on your paycheque than dollars available to meet those demands? If you do, you're not alone. Many parents with young children find themselves short on cash and long on financial obligations.

You don't have to be a rocket scientist to figure out why. I mean, just stop and consider the number of financial balls that you're trying to keep in the air. At this stage in your life, you're probably still paying for your house. You might even have a car loan or two. You've got tons of kid-related expenses to worry about—clothes, shoes, books, toys, sports registration fees, college or university tuition fees, and more—and there's always some sort of emergency cropping up to eat away at whatever savings you've managed to squirrel away in the bank. As if that weren't enough to contend with, you've probably suffering from a chronic case of RESP and/or RRSP guilt, an all-too-common affliction that is caused by the failure to max out one's RESP and/or RRSP contributions year after year.

The number of people contributing to RRSPs increases with age. According to Statistics Canada, barely 10 percent of people under age of 24 contribute to an RRSP as compared to almost half of 45 to 54 year olds.

Source: *The Globe and Mail.*

What's wrong with this picture?

At times you may wonder if you're some sort of financial misfit. You may begin to believe that yours is the only Canadian family that isn't managing to pay off its mortgage ten years early, contribute regularly to its RESP and RRSP plans, and still find the necessary funds to dress its children in designer jeans and make annual treks to the Mother of All Family Vacation Spots, Disneyland.

Here's some news that should help to reassure you. Despite what you may have gathered from watching all those glitzy advertisements during RRSP season, "having it all" is not the norm. While Canadians do have an enviable standard of living, very few of us live in monster homes with three-car garages, and those of us who do manage take glitzy vacations to high-priced tourist destinations often do so with a little help from the nice people at Mastercard and VISA.

It's funny, isn't it? We spend hours explaining to our kids that what they're seeing on TV isn't real—but then we fall into the same trap ourselves by falling prey to those slick financial planning ads that run during RRSP season. Despite what the mutual fund company marketers would have you believe, "real" families—as opposed to those unreasonable facsimiles you'll see on TV—soon learn that financial planning is a matter of making choices and setting priorities: of deciding if that trip to Disneyland is more important to the family than contributing to Junior's college fund. If you can't "have it all"—and frankly that's the case for most of us—you might as well take time to decide what you'd like to have.

Facts and Figures

According to Statistics Canada, 74 percent of tax filers with incomes of $80,000 or more contributed to an RRSP in 1993 as compared to just 31 percent of those with incomes between $20,000 and $30,000.

Source: The Vanier Institute of the Family, *From The Kitchen Table to the Boardroom Table*

Taking a step back

Up until this point in the book, we've been mainly focussing on the here and now: how much money you need to bring home each week to cover your day-to-day expenses. While that's very important—after all, you're not going to get very far in saving for that trip to Disneyland if your family can't even afford to buy groceries—budgeting is only a small part of the financial planning puzzle. You need to take a step back and look at the big picture.

Remember back in the late '80s and early '90s how companies spent huge amounts of time and money hiring high-priced consultants to come up with glitzy mission statements and help them to establish corporate goals? That's kind of what financial planning is all about—although without the high-priced help. While you probably won't want to write some nauseating mission statement for your family, you should at least have an idea about where your family's values lie, since your values should play an important role in determining your financial game plan. Here are a few questions to get you thinking:

1. How important is it to you that one parent leave the workforce to stay at home with the children until they reach a certain age?

2. How important is it to you to be able to pay for your child's education when the time comes?

3. How important is it to you that you get away for a few days each year so that you can spend time together as a family?

4. How important is it to you that you have funds on hand to spend on recreational activities like hockey, skiing, snowboarding, boating, and so on?

5. How important is it to you that you have the funds needed to retire early or enjoy a higher-than-average standard of living during your retirement years?

6. How important is it to you to get rid of any consumer debt (credit cards, car loans, lines of credit, and so on) that you're carrying right now?

7. How important is it to you that you pay off your mortgage sooner rather than later?

8. How important is it to you that you give something back to your community through charitable donations?

You already know from our earlier discussion that couples don't always agree on money, so it's important to find out where your partner's financial priorities lie, too. If you find that you have conflicting priorities, you'll need to figure out a way that the two of you can reach a compromise. If, for example, one partner feels that it's very important to budget for an annual family vacation, while the other partner would prefer to use those funds to pay down the mortgage, you're going to have some financial wheeling and dealing to do! Fortunately, if you're sufficiently creative and willing to compromise, you should be able to come up with a workable solution. You might, for example, decide to take an inexpensive family vacation so that you will have some funds left to put down against the mortgage—or you might decide to put all of your spare cash against the mortgage this year and hit Disneyland next year instead.

If you're lucky, there won't be too much to negotiate. You'll discover that you and your partner are basically on the same wavelength when it comes to your financial goals. This was the case for Anne, a 40-year-old mother of three, and her partner, Andreas: "We have a loose financial plan that includes saving money for retirement, saving for our children's education, living comfortably and enjoyably now, and being able to afford what gives us pleasure. We agreed on these priorities from day one."

Money Talk

"Right now, our priorities are to pay off our credit cards and bank loan and save up enough to have a downpayment for a house within a year. As for more long-term priorities, we want to save for Isabel's college education and accumulate some substantial retirement savings. But right now, the next two to three years is where most of our focus is. We are just starting to get to the point where we are not living from paycheque to paycheque."
— *Stephanie, 26, mother of one.*

Kristin and Jeff, 30-year-old parents with one child, are also in agreement about their family's financial goals. "Our financial goals are to pay off our mortgage by age 40; to give our children the opportunity to participate in extracurricular activities, take family vacations, and the like; to save for our retirement (between age 55 and 60); and to save for our children's education. Basically, we want it all and we are grappling with how to make it all happen. We recently came to the realization that paying off our house is a big factor in achieving the rest of our goals, so it has become our top financial priority."

Leigh, 31, a mother of two, says that she and her partner, Thomas, 30, have structured their financial lives in order to accommodate their shared desire to have her stay at home to raise their children. "One of the main financial priorities for our family is to make it possible for me to continue to stay home with the kids," she explains. "We also strive to save money for our retirement and our children's education. Money comes out of our account every month for these things, so we don't really have to think about them. There are more things we would like to be able to do right now, but they will just have to wait. We both agree that the most important thing is for me to be at home with the kids."

Some couples, like Fiona, 32, and Christopher, 35, parents of six children, find that there's a fair bit of negotiating involved at first. "Initially, as a couple, we needed to refine our priorities, to clearly define where we were going, and the steps we would take to get there. This was not always easy as our financial backgrounds were somewhat dissimilar. Lots of discussions, debates, and compromises were required in order for us to come to a meeting of the pocketbooks. It was made easier, however, by knowing that we wanted a rural home, a simple-back-to-basics type of lifestyle, and a way of living that was in harmony with nature. Our priorities at this time are to create alternative energy sources for our home (such as a wood stove, solar power) so that part of our savings can go toward this end. We are also planning on purchasing a large acreage within the next five years, and this is a financial savings priority as well."

Some couples find that their priorities evolve over time. "For the past few years, we have been focussed on debt reduction," says David, a 38-year-old father of two. "Our total debt from leftover student loans, furniture purchases, household renovations, car payments, et cetera, seemed to be increasing rather than decreasing. Some of our other priorities, now that we are getting our debt under control, include making RRSP contributions to secure our future, making RESP investments to pay for our children's education, travelling to interesting places, and paying for our children's extra-curricular activities such as karate and swimming."

Thinking of using the services of a financial planner? Make sure that he or she complies with the code of ethics set out by the Canadian Association of Financial Planners, which requires that financial planners disclose any potential conflicts of interest, respect their clients' right to confidentiality, and otherwise conduct themselves in a professional manner. To find out more about the association's code of ethics, download a copy of the full document from the organization's Web site at **www.cafp.org** or request a copy from the Canadian Association of Financial Planners, Suite 1710, 439 University Avenue, Toronto, Ontario M5G 1Y8; (416) 593-6592 or 1-800-346-2237; fax (416) 593-8459; or e-mail planners@cafp.org

Walking the talk

Once you've agreed upon your financial priorities and ranked them in order of importance, you're ready to come up with an action plan that will help you to achieve them. While you might be tempted to skip this step because it can be—dare I say it?—a little boring, it's extremely important to persevere. Bribe yourself with chocolate, do your number crunching over a bottle of wine, but do whatever it takes to come up with a written plan that tells you where you're headed and how you're going to get there.

Your plan doesn't have to rival the *Encyclopedia Britannica* in length or complexity. All you really need to do is to list your financial goals in order of importance, figure out how much money you can afford to set aside each month in order to achieve them, and then spell out what your new financial game plan will mean in terms of your monthly budget. Here's how to tackle this task, step by step:

1. List your financial priorities. It's important to be clear about what you're hoping to achieve when writing this financial plan. Do you want to pay off your house in five years, save enough money to allow yourself to retire at age 55, or do something else entirely?

2. Figure out how much money you need to set aside each month to achieve your financial goals. Since you've already analyzed your spending in previous chapters, you should have a pretty good idea about how much extra money you have kicking around, if any. If you don't have any spare cash, you might want to think about cutting back on some of your expenses so that you can set aside money for things that are really important to you—like that annual family getaway or the opportunity to underwrite Junior's Harvard education. Do you need to save $1,000 a month to have a reasonable lifestyle when you retire at age 65, or would $700 a month do the trick? You won't know unless you do the necessary number crunching. There are a number of useful financial planning tools available online that can help to take some of the drudgery out of this particular part of the financial planning process. Check out the tool sections of both iMoney (**www.imoney.com**) and Quicken Canada (**www. quicken.ca**) and you'll find financial planning calculators galore.

3. Divvy up the funds. If debt reduction is your number one priority—and it's pretty close to the top of the list for most couples with young children—then you may decide to slap every spare cent in your budget against your credit card balance. If, on the other hand, your goals are to save for both your children's education and your own retirement, you'll have to figure out how much money you can afford to put into each pot.

4. Adjust your monthly budget accordingly. There's no point in having grandiose visions of spending your retirement years on a yacht or of watching each of your magnificent offspring graduate from Ivy League universities unless you're willing to start working toward these goals today. Make sure that your day-to-day budget reflects your new financial priorities.

Five

Home Is Where the Mortgage Is

To buy or rent: that is the question. Rather than allowing that classic late-third-trimester nesting urge spur you to get in touch with your friendly neighbourhood real estate agent, it's important to stop and carefully weigh the pros and cons of home ownership first. Despite what you may have been told by well-meaning friends and relatives, home ownership isn't necessarily for everyone. Here are a few points to consider before you decide whether or not to take the plunge:

Facts and Figures

Hoping to join the International Order of Mortgage Holders? You're certainly in good company. According to a recent article in *The Globe and Mail,* 25 percent of Canadians who responded to a Royal Bank of Canada housing survey indicated that they intend to purchase a home at some point during the next two years. The percentage for 25 to 34 year olds was even higher: an astounding 40 percent.

- Buying a home isn't always a wise investment. Consider what happened to thousands of homeowners living in Western Canada during the early 1980s. Many of them lost their houses—and their life savings—when housing prices dropped by 29 percent overnight. While housing market crashes like these are rare, they can and do occur. That's why it's important to realize that buying a house is a long-term investment that may not pay off over the short-term. Consider what money expert Elaine Wyatt has to say about this issue in her book *The Money Companion:* "Over time, owning your own home is a good investment. But day-to-day political and economic change can create havoc in the housing market. If you're forced to sell when prices are down, your home could be the most expensive mistake you ever make." The moral of the story? Home ownership is anything but a get-rich-quick scheme.

Table 5.1. Changes in real estate prices, 1990–1998

Wondering how the real estate market in your neck of the woods has done during the 1990s? Here's what's happened to real estate prices in fourteen Canadian communities since 1990.

Victoria	+42%
Vancouver	+26%
Edmonton	+12%
Calgary	+25%
Saskatoon	+44%
Regina	+25%
Winnipeg	+4%
Toronto	−21%
Ottawa	+12%
Montreal	−7%
Moncton	+3%
Charlottetown	+9%
Halifax	+2%
St. John's, Nfld	−2%

Source: *Maclean's Guide to Personal Finance 1999.*

- **Home ownership tends to tie you down—something that you may or may not be ready for at this point in your life.** If you're still hoping to make some significant career moves that might require you to locate across the country or around the world, then it may not be the best time for you to put down roots in the form of a house and mortgage. Most experts agree that you shouldn't even consider purchasing a house unless you are going to be able to live in it for at least three years—preferably five or more. This is because your house needs to increase in value by approximately 10 percent to offset the costs associated with buying and selling a home.

- **Home ownership requires a lot of time, energy, and worry.** When you rent a home, it's your landlord's problem if your furnace packs it in at 3:00 a.m. on the coldest day of the year. When you own a home, it's your problem.

- **Home ownership is expensive.** Mortgage payments can take a huge bite out of your take-home pay. If you love to travel or you have expensive hobbies and interests that you enjoy, you might not be willing to make the financial sacrifices necessary to buy a house.

Of course, it's not all gloom-and-doom on the home ownership front.

If you get lucky and purchase a home that increases in value, you could find yourself significantly further ahead financially because of your decision to own rather than rent.

There's also the satisfaction that comes from knowing that you own a piece of land and the building that sits on it, and that you no longer have to worry about handing a rent cheque over to some landlord. (Of course, the bank that holds your mortgage is kind of like a landlord. But at least the bank doesn't drop by unannounced and hassle you for letting your car drip oil onto the driveway or for playing your music too loudly!)

As you can see, there's no magic formula that you can use to determine whether or not it makes sense for you to buy a home. Only you can decide whether you're willing to make the lifestyle sacrifices necessary to scrape together that down payment and to make those weekly or monthly payments to the bank year in and year out, since that, in a nutshell, is what home ownership is all about.

Show Me the Money!

The best things in life are free—well, at least occasionally. Here are two terrific home-buying guides that are yours for the asking: *Homebuying Step by Step: II A Consumer Guide and Workbook,* by the Canadian Mortgage and Housing Corporation (CMHC), can be ordered free of charge by calling 1-800-668-2642. You can also download the publication from CHMC's Web site, **www.cmhc-schl.gc.ca/**. Order *Mortgage Wise,* by the Canadian Banker's Association, by calling 1-800-263-0231 or by filling out the order form on the association's Web site: **www.cba.ca**

The biggest home-buying mistakes—and how to avoid them

It's one thing to make a financial *faux pas* when you're shopping for a car. It's quite another to make the same sort of mistake when you're buying a house. After all, a financial error on this scale could end up haunting you for a very long time.

Here are some of the most common mistakes that homebuyers make and what you can do to avoid them:

- **Getting your heart set on a particular property.** Once you fall in love with a particular property, it's game over. Your ability to think logically goes out the window and you may find yourself making some very poor decisions. Even if your heart is doing flip-flops at the prospect of owning the property you've just seen, force yourself to put on the brakes before you decide whether or not to put in an offer.

- **Mixing up your family's needs with its wants.** It's easy to be seduced by Jacuzzis, French doors, skylights, and other bells and whistles—items that can significantly push the purchase price of a home beyond what you can reasonably afford to pay.

Money Talk

"Keep your family's long-term financial goals in mind. If you are both currently working and want to eventually have one of you be a stay-at-home parent, make sure you can handle the mortgage on one income."
- *Susan, 34, mother of two.*

- **Failing to take your family's long-term plans into consideration.** If you're planning to add to your family, make sure that you buy a house with a sufficient number of bedrooms. Moving is an expensive proposition, so you don't want to force yourself to do it again in another couple of year's time, just because you lacked the foresight to buy a four-bedroom home.
- **Overextending yourself by buying an overly expensive house.** If you borrow the maximum amount of money that the bank is willing to lend you, you could be in for a rude shock: there might not be enough money in your budget to pay for anything but the bare essentials. This is fine if you're prepared to be house poor for at least a few years, but it can be the cause of much pain and suffering if you're not anticipating the dramatic lifestyle changes that typically accompany a huge mortgage.
- **Failing to consider the long-term resale potential of the home.** While you might not have any problem buying a house that backs onto the runway of a major airport, you might have a hard time finding a buyer for the property when you eventually decide to sell.

What to do before you call your lender

There's an art to making your way through the mortgage maze and cutting yourself the best possible deal. Here are seven steps to take before you start filling out that mortgage application.

1. Do your homework. Research interest rates, mortgage features, the housing markets, and anything else that might help you to save money on your home or mortgage.

the Bottom line

"Be sure to check out the demographics of the neighbourhood. Is it a young neighbourhood or is it more 'mature'? You want to make sure that it's a good fit with your stage in life. Be sure to check out the location of schools if you have or are planning to have children. You'll also want to consider such factors as the accessibility to shopping and community resources and to consider the future growth patterns of the area."
- *Kristin, 30, mother of one.*

2. Learn how to speak the language—the language of the mortgage industry, that is! If you're not fully up to speed on terms like amortization, you've never even heard about the RRSP Home Buyer's Plan, and you haven't got a clue about the difference between a conventional and high-ratio mortgage, perhaps it's time to read through the glossary at the end of this book.

3. Analyze your financial situation. Make sure you have a clear idea about how much house you can—and can't—afford (see below).

4. Come up with a wish list for your mortgage. Which features are most important to you: the ability to prepay portions of your mortgage, the ability to take your mortgage with you if you move, or something else entirely?

5. Prepare to make the best possible case to the lender at your financial institution. Anticipate the types of information you'll be asked to provide (see pages 93 and 94) and arm yourself with the numbers you'll need to fill out the mortgage application thoroughly and accurately. (Nothing shakes a potential lender's confidence more than watching a mortgage applicant underestimate his or her personal debt to the tune of $20,000!)

6. Check out your credit report. You don't want to go through the trauma of having your mortgage application turned down because of an error on your credit report. (You might want to flip back to Chapter 2 for details on how to obtain a copy of your credit report.)

7. Tap into the mortgage grapevine. Find out where your friends have their mortgages, how happy they are with their lenders, and whether they were able to negotiate for any added bells and whistles (e.g., a cut in the mortgage rate).

How much house can you afford?

Once you and your partner have decided that you would like to buy a house, the first order of business is to figure out how much house you can afford. After all, there's no point house shopping in Cadillac neighbourhoods if you're limited to a Lada price range!

Before we go any further, I think it's important to remind you of one of the deepest and darkest secrets of the financial world: there's a huge difference between the amount the bank thinks you can afford to borrow and the level of debt you can carry without breaking out into a cold sweat. So when you work through the calculations below, it's important to keep in mind that we're talking about maximums here. You don't have to borrow the whole amount. In fact, you probably shouldn't. Frankly, you'll be under a lot less stress if you give yourself some breathing room financially.

Money Talk

"I have always found that the banks are willing to lend me far more money that I think I should borrow. We have tried to keep our mortgage to less than 75 percent of what the banks would lend us, particularly since we are currently in a period of low interest rates, and if interest rates were to increase significantly, I wouldn't want to be put in a position where I couldn't afford the mortgage payments."
- *David, 38, father of two.*

There's no such thing as one size fits all.

One of the problems with the bank's methods of assessing your ability to shoulder debt is the fact that the formulas used generally fail to take into account such factors as your financial goals and what type of lifestyle you hope to enjoy. If, for example, you're determined to maximize your RRSP contributions, you won't have as much money to pour into mortgage payments as someone who's decided that retirement saving is a low priority at this stage in his or her life. Similarly, if you can't imagine making it through a long Canadian winter without at least one week-long escape to Florida, you're going to have to knock down your mortgage payments a bit so you'll still have the funds needed to fund your annual midwinter getaway.

Bottom line?

You're the only one who can make an educated decision about what you can reasonably afford to borrow. Don't be tempted to download that responsibility to anyone else, especially someone who stands to make money on the transaction!

How the bank decides how much to lend you

It's a little disconcerting to watch some bank employee you've never met in your life punch some numbers into a spreadsheet and then tell you how much you can—or can't—borrow. You may feel a bit more comfortable with the whole process of applying for a mortgage if you do a little number crunching of your own ahead of time. Here's what you need to know.

Banks and other lenders look at two figures when determining how much money they should lend you: your gross debt-service ratio (housing costs) and your total debt-service ratio (your housing costs plus all of your consumer debt—things like credit cards payments, car loans, lines of credit, and so on). The bank likes your gross debt-service ratio to stay under 32 percent of your total gross household income and your total debt-service ratio to stay under 40 percent.

What many first-time home-buyers don't realize is that the gross debt-service ratio figure is made up of more than just your mortgage payments. In addition to the mortgage principal and interest that you are paying, it also takes into account your property taxes and your heating bills, and—should you decide to buy a condominium—half of your monthly condominium fees as well. Obviously, these other types of expenses take a big bite out of your gross debt-service ratio, dramatically reducing the funds available for your mortgage principal and interest payments.

Looking for a house you can afford

It's a good idea to look at houses that are priced somewhat lower than the maximum you can afford. That way, if your real estate agent happens to come across the home of your dreams and it's only a thousand dollars or so over the budget range you gave him or her, you might still be able to afford to buy it. A good rule of thumb is to chop 5 percent off the amount you can afford to spend on a house and then check out properties in that price range. In other words, if you can afford a $200,000 home, start looking in the $190,000 price range instead.

You can get a rough idea of the amount of money you can afford to spend on mortgage payments—at least, in your financial institution's opinion—by working your way through the calculations in Table 5.2.

Table 5.2: Your maximum affordable mortgage payment

Step 1	Calculate your gross monthly income by adding together your employment income, your partner's employment income, and any other sources of income.	_____
Step 2	Multiply this figure by 32% to calculate the amount. of money you can afford to spend on housing-related costs each month. This is Figure A	_____
Step 3	Find out how much you could expect to pay each year for property taxes and heating costs for the property that you're considering. (If this information is unavailable, ask your real estate agent or lender to help you to estimate these costs or call the local property tax department.) Divide this annual cost by 12 to obtain your monthly cost. If you're planning to purchase a condominium, you will need to add in 50% of the cost of your monthly condominium fees, too.) This is Figure B.	_____
Step 4	Subtract Figure B from Figure A. The result represents the maximum mortgage payment you can afford to make each month, provided, of course, that your consumer debt doesn't take any more than 8% of your gross monthly household income, in which case it would start eating into your housing budget, too.	_____

Now that you know how much you can afford to spend on mortgage payments, you can figure out how big a mortgage you can afford to carry. Simply look up the monthly payment factor for the interest rate and amortization you're considering (see Table 5.3) and then use this mortgage payment factor to figure out how much money you can afford to borrow. Example:

You are considering taking out a mortgage with an interest rate of 8 percent and an amortization period of 25 years. You can afford to pay about $1,140 per month in mortgage principal and interest payments.

Step 1: Find the correct mortgage factor for the mortgage you are considering. In this case, the correct figure is 7.632.

Step 2: Take the $1,140 you can afford to spend each month and divide it by the mortgage factor. Then multiply this figure by 1,000 to figure out the maximum amount of money you will be able to borrow. $1,140 divided by 7.632 = $149.37 x 1,000 = $149,371. Add to this figure the amount of money that you've managed to squirrel away towards your down payment less your anticipated housing-related expenses (see discussion below) and you'll have a pretty good idea of how much money you can afford to spend on a house.

Table 5.3: Mortgage Payment Table

The following table shows the monthly payment factor of principal and interest for each $1,000 of mortgage. For example, the monthly principal and interest payment for a 25-year $100,000 mortgage at 8% interest is 7.632. ($100,000 divided by $1,000) x 7.632 = $763.20. Your monthly mortgage payment on a mortgage this size would be $763.20.

Rate (%)	25 years	20 years	15 years	10 years
6.0	6.398	7.122	8.399	11.065
6.5	6.698	7.405	8.664	11.311
7.0	7.004	7.693	8.932	11.559
7.5	7.316	7.986	9.205	11.810
8.0	7.632	8.284	9.482	12.064
8.5	7.954	8.586	9.762	12.320
9.0	8.280	8.892	10.045	12.579
9.5	8.610	9.202	10.332	12.840
10	8.945	9.517	10.623	13.103
10.5	9.283	9.835	10.916	13.369
11	9.625	10.156	11.213	13.637

Closing costs

It's a lesson that many first-time home buyers learn the hard way: there are a lot of hidden costs involved in buying a home. Here's a list of some of the major types of expenses you can expect to pay before you walk out of your lawyer's office with the keys to your new house in hand:

- GST. If you purchase a new home that is worth $450,000 or more, you will be required to pay 7 percent GST on the cost of the house. If your new house costs less than that, you are eligible for a 2.5 percent rebate, which will bring your GST expense down to 4.5 percent. The best way to save money on the GST, however, is to purchase a resale home rather than a brand spanking new one: unless the home has been substantially renovated, you don't have to pay any GST.

- **Provincial fees.** It's not enough to fork over big chunks of cash to the federal government, of course. The provincial government also wants its cut! You can expect to pay $100 or more to have your provincial government register your mortgage and transfer your property title. This charge usually shows up on your legal bill.
- **Land transfer tax.** Applicable in most parts of Canada, the land transfer tax will set you back anywhere from one to four percent of the purchase price of the property.
- **Appraisal fee.** Your lender may require that you pay for an appraisal on the home that you are purchasing. You can expect to pay between $150 and $250 for this document.
- **Survey fee.** Unless the vendor is able to provide you with a copy of a recent survey that is acceptable to the lender, you should plan to set aside $500 or so to have a new survey prepared. Note: Some lenders are willing to waive the survey requirement if you have title insurance (a type of insurance that protects your investment if there is a problem with the title to your house).
- **Property insurance.** Your lender will want to see proof that you have arranged to have your new house insured—its way of protecting its investment in the event that your home burns to the ground.

the Bottom line

When you're shopping around for house insurance, be sure to let the broker know if your home will be equipped with a home security system, a sprinkler system, or other safety features. Often something as simple as having a fire extinguisher in your kitchen can save you money.

- **Prepaid taxes or utilities.** You may have to reimburse the vendor if certain bills (e.g., hydro, water, gas, or property taxes) have been prepaid beyond the closing date.
- **Service charges.** Whether you are buying a new home or a used home, you can expect to spend a small fortune on hook-up charges for such services as water, gas, hydro, cable, and telephone. There's not much

you can do about these charges, unfortunately, other than simply fork over the necessary cash.

- **Lawyer's fees.** Most purchasers choose to hire a lawyer to review the offer to purchase, to search the title of the new property, to draw up mortgage documents, and to tend to closing details. The going rate for a simple lawyer-assisted real estate transaction is $500 or more.
- **Mortgage loan insurance premium and application fee.** If you have a high-ratio mortgage and you decide to insure your mortgage through Canada Mortgage and Housing Corporation (CMHC), you can expect to pay a premium of 0.5 to 3.75 percent of the total value of the mortgage plus an application fee of $75 ($235 if you don't have a valid house appraisal). Note: If you're going for a conventional mortgage, your lender may offer to sell you mortgage insurance. This type of insurance tends to be quite expensive. In most cases, you're better off boosting your life insurance coverage instead.
- **Moving costs.** You will pay between $50 to $100 an hour for a van with three movers.

Show Me the Money!

Don't want to move all that baby stuff and furniture on your own? If you pick the right closing date, you can save yourself hundreds of dollars on the costs of hiring a professional mover. Movers tend to charge 10 to 20 percent more during their busiest periods—the beginning and end of each month and during June, July, and August.

- **An estoppel certificate.** If you're buying a condominium in any province other than Ontario, you will need to supply an estoppel certificate, a document that describes a condominium corporation's financial and legal status. You should budget approximately $50 for the estoppel certificate and the necessary supporting documents.
- **Condominium fees.** Here's another fee that condominium owners need to be prepared for: the monthly maintenance charge for the common areas in a condominium complex. You can expect to be asked to come up with at least a couple of hundred dollars at the time of closing, possibly considerably more.
- **A home inspection fee.** You can expect to pay anywhere from $150 to $500 for the services of a professional home inspector—a small price to pay if it prevents you from picking up a property like the one in the hit

1980s movie, *The Money Pit.* Note: If the home inspector recommends major structural repairs such as a new roof, you'll either want to factor these costs into the price of buying this particular home or walk away from the home entirely.

- **Water quantity and quality certificate.** If you're buying a rural property, your lender will ask you to pay the cost of certifying the quantity and quality of the water—typically $50 to $100.

- **Real estate fees.** Unless you go with a discount real estate broker or sell your home privately, you can expect to pay 5 or 6 percent in real estate fees. (The going rate is 8 percent in Quebec). Note: These are costs that you can expect to pay if you're selling a home at the same time as buying a new one. You won't be on the hook for real estate fees if you're the buyer—at least not directly!

Show Me the Money!

"Always shop around for the best mortgage rates. You don't have to have all your banking needs met by one institution."
- *Laura, 30, mother of one* .

Where the money is

Now that you've figured out roughly how much you would like to borrow, your next step is to figure out who you would like to borrow the money from. As you can see from Table 5.4, there are a large number of players in the Canadian mortgage business: banks, trust companies, caisses populaires, credit unions, finance companies, pension funds, and private lenders (including family members). If you don't qualify for conventional financing because of a shaky credit history or other problem, you might decide to use the services of a mortgage broker instead of approaching lenders directly. (Note: in most cases, the mortgage broker's fee is paid by the lender.)

Table 5.4: Where the mortgage money comes from

	1994	1995	1996	1997	1998
			($ millions)		
Total	324,036	336,126	349,862	368,707	386,941
Chartered banks	164,940	177,079	191,341	213,350	231,986
Trust and mortgage loan companies	44,898	41,954	39,749	31,538	22,374
Credit unions and caisses populaires	44,414	46,169	48,231	50,768	52,194
Life insurance companies	20,621	21,148	21,719	21,374	20,084
Pension funds	8,185	8,007	7,724	7,983	7,978
Finance companies and other institutions	24,340	24,476	25,060	26,530	26,928
NHA mortgage-backed securities (held by groups of investors)	16,637	17,225	15,614	14,157	17,311

Source: Statistics Canada.

Regardless of what type of lender you decide to approach, you'll likely be asked to supply a lot of information and/or documentation, including

- personal information (age, marital status, dependents, current and previous addresses)
- details of employment, including proof of income (T4 slips, personal income tax returns, recent pay stub, or a letter form your employer stating your position and your income)
- details about other sources of income (pensions or rental income, for example)
- copies of RRSP statements, GIC certificates, and other financial documents
- copies of life insurance policies
- details about your current banking arrangements and copies of your bank statements for the previous three months
- copies of your most recent credit card statements (and/or a list of outstanding balances and monthly payments)
- evidence that you have accumulated the necessary down payment
- a letter from any relative who has given you money (to demonstrate that the money in question was actually a gift and not a loan)

- a list of your assets, including property and vehicles
- a list of your liabilities, including credit card balances and car loans, that specifies both the total balance owing and the amount of your monthly payments
- copies of rent cheques written to your landlord during the previous 12 months
- a copy of the property listing
- a copy of the Agreement of Purchase and Sale on a resale home (and possibly a copy of the front and back of the deposit cheque that you wrote to the vendor)
- a set of plans and cost estimates for a new home
- a copy of the listing agreement if you're selling the home you own right now (or a copy of the Agreement of Purchase and Sale if the home has already been sold)
- a copy of the condominium's financial statements if you're purchasing a condominium
- a certificate demonstrating that the well and septic system are operational (where applicable)
- mortgage insurance fees if a high-ratio mortgage is required
- fees for an appraisal (or copy of a recent appraisal report, if one is available) and
- permission for the lender to do a credit check on you and/or your partner.

If you and/or your partner are self-employed, you will also be asked to bring along copies of your business financial statements and your income tax returns for the past few years so that the lender can see how much income you actually manage to take home and how stable your earnings are from year to year.

Show Me the Money!

Planning to rent out the basement of your new home to bring in some extra cash? While it sounds like a good way to help with the mortgage payments, it could be a recipe for financial disaster. Municipal by-laws in many areas prohibit basement apartments. Do your homework ahead of time so that you don't get hit with any surprises.

When to apply

You don't have to wait until you're ready to make an offer on a particular property before you apply for a mortgage. In fact, it's a good idea to get preapproved for a mortgage before you start looking because it will allow you to move more quickly once you're ready to make an offer.

When you are preapproved for a mortgage, the lender gives you a letter that specifies the amount that you have been approved for and the interest rate that will apply. (Note: If rates decline after you are preapproved for your mortgage but before the property deal closes, you should be able to get the lender to arrange the mortgage at the lower rate.) Mortgage preapproval is generally valid for 60 to 90 days.

Hold on before you start packing your bags, however. The mortgage isn't actually a done deal until you obtain a satisfactory appraisal on the property and pass a credit check. That's the bank's method of insuring that neither you nor the property in question are lemons!

Money Talk

"With a pre-approved mortgage, you can make an offer on a property without making the offer conditional on financing, since you've already obtained approval for your mortgage. This can work in your favour, since most vendors prefer unconditional offers. It can work against you, however, if you sign an agreement to purchase the property and your lender decides that you've offered too much money."
Source: Gordon Pape, The Canadian Mortgage Book.

Do-it-yourself financing

If you're a first-time home buyer, there's another source of mortgage money that you should know about: your own RRSP.

Under the federal government's RRSP Home Buyer's Plan, you are permitted to withdraw up to $20,000 from your RRSP to buy or build a qualifying home without incurring the usual tax penalties on the amount withdrawn.

As with any other tax break, there's some fine print you need to know about:

- The home that you will be purchasing must be in Canada, and it must be your principal residence. (In other words, it can't be a vacation property or a property that you have purchased for investment purposes.)

- You must enter into a written agreement to buy or build a qualifying home.
- The funds in question must have been in your RRSP for at least 90 days before you make a Home Buyer's Plan withdrawal.
- You can't make a contribution to your RRSP in the year that you withdraw funds under the plan—something that can prevent you from taking advantage of one of the best tax breaks, unfortunately.
- You must repay a minimum of 1/15 of the amount that you "borrow" from your RRSP each year until this "loan" has been fully repaid. If you default on one of your payments, the government treats that year's portion of the repayment as taxable income, which can result in a major tax hit for you come April 30 of the following year.

While the RRSP Home Buyer's Plan is a great idea in principle, it has one major drawback: the plan forces you to choose between saving for your retirement and buying a home. So before you dash to the bank to take advantage of the program, you need to think long and hard about the long-term costs of taking those funds out of your RRSP. (You'll find a more detailed discussion of the advantages of RRSPs elsewhere in this book.) Unless you're confident that your house is going to appreciate quickly enough to make up for the hit to your retirement savings, you might want to think about finding your mortgage money someplace else.

Facts and Figures

Here's a little mortgage trivia that you can use to impress your friends. Banks weren't allowed to lend money for mortgages until 1954, when the federal Bank Act was revised. Today, they're the prime source of mortgage money in Canada, with the nine largest banks accounting for more than 59 percent of the $386 billion mortgage market in Canada.
Sources: Statistics Canada; Gordon Pape, *The Canadian Mortgage Book.*

All in the family

Borrowing money from family members might seem like the ideal solution to your mortgage woes, but it could end up being the biggest financial mistake you ever make. More often than not, there are hidden strings attached to that loan—strings that you might not find out about until it's too late.

Don't follow what I'm saying? Allow me to give you a hypothetical example.

Your parents lend you $50,000 towards the down payment on your first house. You're ecstatic at first, and so are they. After all, there are few things more exciting than becoming a home owner for the very first time—unless, of course, it's becoming the proud parents of a first-time home buyer!

You no sooner move into your new digs when you decide that you'd like to do a little redecorating. That red plush carpet in the rec room is hideous, to say the least, and you could definitely live without the lime green fixtures in the downstairs bathroom. Before you know it, you've pumped $5,000 into renovations. You invite the folks over to see the products of your labour, and you're surprised by their lack of enthusiasm. They aren't happy that you've given the Rec Room From Hell a new life: they're mad that you spent "their" money on something that they see as frivolous and unnecessary. After all, if the circa-1965 orange shag rug in their rec room is good enough for them, why shouldn't the red rug be good enough for you? And besides, if you've got that kind of money to burn, why aren't you offering to pay them back a little sooner? Perhaps it was a mistake for them to lend you this money in the first place...

Money Talk

The Internet is a home buyer's dream come true. Find up-to-the minute information on mortgage rates at Cannex Canada, (**www.cannex.com/canada/**). Search for a realtor or check out properties at the MLS Web site (**www.mls.ca**) or check out the Web sites of real estate organizations such as Remax (**www.remax.ca**), Royal LePage (**www.royallepage.com**), Century 21 (**www.century21.com**), and Coldwell Banker (**www.coldwellbanker.com**). You can find mortgage calculators on the Web sites of most the major banks. If you're looking for one that offers eye-catching graphs and other bells and whistles, there's only one place to go: to the Canada Mortgage Web site (**www.CanMortgage.com**).

While it's impossible to find statistics on the number of family relationships destroyed by loan-related woes, I'd be willing to wager a bet that it's a fairly significant number, just judging by the number of couples I know personally who have horror stories of their own to tell. If, however, you are determined to ignore my advice and take whatever money your parents or other relatives are ready to throw your way, at least make an effort to do things the right way. Here are a few tips.

- Find out what types of strings are attached to the money before you agree to take the loan or gift. Will the relatives who are lending you the money expect you to live like paupers until the loan is repaid? Will they expect you to repay them for their generous gift by supporting them in their old age?

- Be clear about how long your parents are willing to lend you the money. Do they expect to be paid back in full the next time your mortgage rolls over or are they willing to lend you the money for a longer period of time?

- Make sure you and your parents agree on a payment schedule. Don't settle for some vague agreement that you will repay the money "when you can afford it." (That day may never come, given the huge number of expenses that you'll likely be faced with during your first couple of years of home ownership; and you may have some royally ticked off relatives to contend with in the meantime.) Instead, specify the date upon which you will start repaying the loan and how much your payments will be. Then put all of these details in writing.

- Talk about what would happen to the loan in the event that you or your partner were to die unexpectedly. If you died, would your spouse be expected to pay back the loan from the proceeds of your life insurance policy? If your parents died, how would the loan be handled by their estate?

- Figure out how your siblings feel about the arrangement. Are they completely okay with the arrangement or are they treating this as further proof that Dad always liked you best?

- Ask yourself if you're taking on more debt than you can handle. It's one thing to take out a $150,000 mortgage on a $200,000 home. It's quite another to take out that same mortgage if you've also got to make payments on a $50,000 loan from Mom and Dad!

- Resist the temptation to lie on your mortgage application. Your bank could pull the rug out from under your home buying dreams if they find out that the "gift" your parents supposedly gave you is actually a loan. Note: If your mortgage is ensured by Canada Mortgage and Housing Corporation (CMHC), you'll be asked to provide written confirmation that it's a genuine gift, not a loan.

Facts and Figures

The number of people between the ages of 35 and 44 buying homes has declined over the past 15 years. While 73 percent of people in that age bracket owned homes in 1981, only 68 percent of 35 to 44 year olds owned homes in 1996.
Source: Canada Mortgage and Housing Corporation.

- Find out whether your parents will expect you to pay interest on the loan or whether they're simply interested in having you pay back the principal. If they intend to charge you interest, find out what interest rate they have in mind and then make sure that it's competitive with the rates being charged by commercial lenders.

- Be prepared to spend some money on legal fees if your parents agree to carry your mortgage for you. An I.O.U. on a scrap of paper simply doesn't cut it when there are significant sums of money involved. It's only reasonable for your parents to ask that you draw up a mortgage or formal promissory note in order to formalize the deal. After all, their life savings are at stake. By going the mortgage route, they'll ensure that they will be treated as secured creditors in the event that you experience an unavoidable financial meltdown caused by job loss, disability, or some other unforeseen disaster.

- If your parents agree to guarantee (co-sign) your mortgage, find out how much of the mortgage they're prepared to guarantee (it can be limited to a specific amount) and how long they're willing to act as guarantors. You should also make sure that they are clear about what they're agreeing to do, just so that there aren't any misunderstandings down the road: in addition to committing to make up any mortgage payments you miss, they're also expressing their willingness to be on the hook for your house insurance and property taxes, too. (Given all that they've done for you, you'd better make a point of getting them something extra special on Mother's Day and Father's Day!)

- If your parents are thinking about borrowing money against their own mortgage so that they can lend this money to you, offer to have a mortgage secured against your own home on identical terms to eliminate any risk of their losing their home. After all, there's only so much you should be prepared to take from relatives—particularly those who are approaching or into their retirement years.

As you can see, you need to think long and hard before you agree to borrow money or accept a substantial gift from relatives. Sure, that interest-free loan may save you money in the short-run, but it's no bargain if it ends up costing you your relationship with your family.

Learning to speak the language of loans

There's no point even trying to deny it. You haven't got a hope of making your way through the mortgage maze unless you've got all your mortgage lingo down pat. Here's a crash course in mortgage speak, just in case you've forgotten what some of the more important terms actually mean.

The types of mortgages

You will find two basic choices on the mortgage menu: conventional mortgages and high-ratio mortgages.

Conventional mortgages require a down payment of 25 percent or more. They cannot, by law, exceed 75 percent of either the appraised value or purchase price of the home, whichever is less.

High-ratio mortgages require less than a 25 percent down payment—typically 10 percent, although qualifying first-time home buyers may be permitted to put down as little as 5 percent. These types of mortgages must be insured by either a private insurer or the Canada Mortgage and Housing Corporation (CMHC). Depending on the size of the loan and the value of the home, CMHC typically charges between 0.5 and 3.75 percent on the full amount of the mortgage in order to insure it against default. The premiums can either be tacked on to the mortgage principal or paid in full at the time of closing.

Show Me the Money!

Don't like financial surprises? Be sure to look into Canada Mortgage and Housing Corporation's Mortgage Rate Protection Program. Designed to protect you against dramatic increases in mortgage rates, the program kicks in if your interest rate jumps by two percent or more when it's time to renew your mortgage. Under the program, you are reimbursed for a portion of the resulting increase in your monthly mortgage payments. To find out more about the Mortgage Rate Protection Program, contact CMHC by calling 1-800-668-2642 or by visiting CMHC's Web site: **www.cmhc-schl.gc.ca**

To qualify for a CMHC insured mortgage, you must meet the following criteria:

- You must be living in Canada.
- The house that you are intending to purchase must be your principal residence.
- Your housing payments including principal, interest, property taxes, heating, and 50 percent of your condominium fees (where applicable) cannot exceed more than 32 percent of your gross household income (a.k.a. your gross debt-service ratio).
- Your total debt load cannot be more that 40 percent of your gross household income (a.k.a. your total debt-service ratio).
- You must meet other criteria as set out by CMHC from time to time.

the Bottom line

Once you get three years into your CMHC mortgage, you can buy your way out by agreeing to pay a three-month interest penalty.

While the vast majority of home buyers go with one of the two types of mortgages described above, there are a few other mortgage options out there, including

- second mortgages (an additional mortgage on a property that already has a first mortgage)
- a Vendor Take Back (VTB) mortgage (the vendor becomes the lender and the purchaser becomes the mortgagee)
- assuming an existing mortgage (the purchaser takes over the vendor's existing mortgage under the terms of the Agreement of Purchase and Sale)
- a leasehold mortgage (a mortgage on a home where the land is leased rather than owned)
- a collateral mortgage (a promissory note that is used to secure mortgages)
- bridge financing (a short-term loan that allows you to carry two mortgages at once when the closing dates on the property you are selling and the property you are buying don't match)

You can find a detailed discussion of these and other mortgage options in *The Canadian Mortgage Book,* by Gordon Pape.

Open or closed?

Another choice you'll be forced to make is whether you would like your mortgage to be open or closed.

If you choose an open mortgage, you will be able to pay off some or all of the outstanding balance at any time without incurring any of the usual interest penalties. Most lenders offer six-month open mortgages, and a few offer one-year open mortgages as well. You can expect to pay a slightly higher interest rate on an open mortgage, but if you are expecting to receive a lump sum of money later in the year that you'll be able to smack down against the mortgage principal, or if you plan to sell your home in the near future, this is definitely the way to go.

If you choose a closed mortgage instead, you'll get a slightly lower interest rate—usually a quarter-percent to a half-percent lower—but you'll lose the ability to pay off your mortgage in full or in part without penalty unless your mortgage happens to have a prepayment feature (see below). This restriction could cost you a small fortune if you ended up moving before the end of the term of your mortgage.

Short term vs. long term

Here's yet another thing to think about: whether you'd like a short-term or long-term mortgage.

Short-term mortgages (e.g., six-month mortgages) offer rates that are consistently lower than the rates for long-term mortgages. What's more, because your mortgage opens up more regularly, you'll have more opportunities to make additional lump sump payments to reduce the principal without incurring any interest penalties.

Long-term mortgages allow you to negotiate a mortgage at a particular interest rate and know that your payments will remain the same for the term of your mortgage (e.g., five years). Such peace of mind doesn't come without a price, however: you can expect to pay anywhere from one to three percent more than the going rate for six-month mortgages. What's more, your peace of mind could quickly disappear if interest rates started to climb and you found your mortgage locked in at an insanely high rate for the next ten years—the very thing that happened to my husband and me!

If you can't decide whether to play the six-month mortgage game or to take the more conservative long-term mortgage approach instead, you might want to do both. Some financial institutions offer multiple-rate (also called split) mortgages. You can negotiate a portion of the total mortgage loan at one rate and term and the balance at another. For example, if you needed to borrow $100,000, you might decide to take out a $30,000 mortgage with a six-month term and five-year amortization and a $70,000 five-year mortgage with a five-year term and a ten-year amortization.

Fixed or variable

You'll also need to decide whether you're interested in a mortgage with a fixed rate (a rate that is locked in for the term of the mortgage) or a variable rate (a rate that is set each month by the lender).

Show Me the Money!

Some lenders offer protected or capped variable rate mortgages, which will allow the interest rate to rise to a only certain level. This feature is definitely worth considering if interest rates are particularly volatile.

With a variable-rate mortgage, your payment is fixed, but the percentage of your money that goes to cover the principal vs. the interest on the mortgage rises and falls along with the rate. It's an attractive option if interest rates are high when you arrange your mortgage, but are expected to fall in the near future. (Note: If they happen to move in the opposite direction instead, you can quickly convert to a fixed-rate mortgage by paying a penalty.)

Just one important bit of fine print on these types of mortgages: if you're getting into your new home by the skin of your teeth, you might not be able to obtain a variable-rate mortgage. Many lenders restrict the amount of money that they're willing to lend you on a mortgage of this type to 70 percent of the purchase price of the home, which gives them a bit of a cushion if the housing market hits a rough patch.

the Bottom line

A convertible mortgage allows you to enjoy the best of both worlds: you get an attractive interest rate now as well as the freedom to lock into a fixed-rate mortgage later if interest rates start to rise. Just make sure that there aren't any restrictions that could limit your options. Some lenders will not allow convertible mortgage holders to convert to short-term mortgages, insisting instead that they lock in to five-year terms.

Amortization

You also need to consider the amortization period that you would like on your mortgage: the amount of time over which your mortgage will be repaid. Obviously, the longer you take to repay your mortgage, the lower your payments will be, but the more interest you will pay in the long run (see Table 5.5).

Table 5.5: Payment comparison over various amortization periods for a $100,000 mortgage at 10% interest

Amortization period	Monthly payment	Total payments	Total interest paid	Interest savings
25 years	$895	$268,500	$168,500	—
20 years	$952	$228,480	$128,480	$40,020
15 years	$1,063	$191,340	$91,340	$77,160
10 years	$1,311	$157,320	$57,240	$111,260

Notes: Figures have been rounded. Figures are based on a constant interest rate for the entire amortization period.

Source: CMHC.

A matter of interest

It definitely pays to shop around when you're in the market for a new mortgage. You could save yourself thousands of dollars in interest and reduce your monthly payments significantly by shaving even a mere quarter-percentage point off your mortgage. (Table 5.6 shows how an increase in interest rates affects your monthly payment.)

If you give the bulk of your business to a particular financial institution—your chequing account, your RRSP, and your credit card business, for example—they may be willing to offer you a preferential rate on a mortgage. The industry term for this special deal is "relationship pricing." If your financial institution isn't willing to cut you a special deal, then shop around. After all, if they don't value your relationship enough to put their money where their mouth is, why should you?

Table 5.6: How interest rates affect your mortgage payment

The following figures are for a $100,000 mortgage amortized over 25 years.

Interest rate (%)	Monthly payment
6.0	$640.00
6.5	$670.00
7.0	$701.00
7.5	$732.00
8.0	$764.00
8.5	$795.00
9.0	$828.00
9.5	$862.00
10.0	$895.00
10.5	$929.00
11.0	$963.00
11.5	$998.00
12.0	$1,032.00
12.5	$1,068.00
13.0	$1103.00

The Brave New World of mortgages

Remember what happened to disposable diapers in the late 1980s? The diaper manufacturers dramatically expanded the number of products they offered virtually overnight. They started offering diapers for girls only, diapers for boys only, and diapers that featured every conceivable bell and whistle short of a computerized moisture detector.

The same phenomenon has occurred in the mortgage industry. There are now hundreds of different types of mortgages to choose from—something that makes finding the right mortgage a heck of a lot more challenging and time-consuming.

Here's what to look for the next time you start shopping around for a mortgage:

- **A partial prepayment option:** Some mortgages allow you to make a partial prepayment against your principal, either through a lump sum payment or by increasing your monthly payment. This can be a terrific way to cut your interest costs, as long as you understand all of the fine print. Some agreements will allow you to make one or more prepayments at any point in the mortgage year, while others will limit you to a one-time lump sum on the anniversary date of your mortgage; and some prepayment options are based on calendar year while others are based on your mortgage renewal date.

- **Portability**: A portability clause allows you to take your mortgage with you without paying any type of interest penalty if you happen to move before your mortgage term expires.

Show Me the Money!

Don't commit to a mortgage term that's greater than the number of years that you're likely to be in your home unless your mortgage has a portability clause. Otherwise, you could find yourself faced with the rather unappealing prospect of buying your way out of your mortgage—something that generally doesn't come cheap.

- **Assumability**: An assumability clause gives you the option of allowing a future purchaser to take over your mortgage payments, which could be a strong selling point if the interest rate on your mortgage ends up being significantly lower than the prevailing interest rate at the time. Of course, you'll definitely want to get some legal advice before you take advantage of your assumability clause. If the person taking over the mortgage didn't meet your lender's usual credit requirements, you could potentially find yourself on the hook for his or her mortgage payments if he or she happened to default.

- **Early renewal**: An early renewal option allows you to renew your mortgage before it matures—a nice feature to be able to take advantage of if mortgage rates are expected to skyrocket in the very near future, but your mortgage doesn't open up for another six months. Just be sure you understand what you're getting yourself into: if the interest rate when you renew is lower than the interest rate on the existing mortgage, you could be asked to pay a hefty interest penalty.

- **Expandability**: An expandability clause gives you the ability to expand the amount of money you have borrowed under a first mortgage at the agreed-upon amount of interest in the event that you need additional funds during the course of the mortgage. This feature is one of the most cost-effective ways to finance a home renovation.

the Bottom line

Is that discount mortgage rate that your home builder is offering really a bargain? Maybe, maybe not. Usually, the home builder makes a lump-sum payment to a particular lender in order to secure you a short-term mortgage (generally six months) at a preferential rate. More often than not, the builder adds this additional charge to the purchase price of your home.

Interest zappers

Looking for ways to minimize the amount of interest you end up paying on your mortgage? Here are some tried-and-true methods of beating the mortgage lenders at their own game:

- Make a larger down payment. It's not rocket science, but it certainly bears repeating: the less money you have to borrow, the less you're going to pay in interest charges.
- Choose the shortest possible amortization on your mortgage. As you can see from Table 5.7, you can save a significant amount of money over the long run by increasing your mortgage payment over the short run.

Table 5.7: The effect of shorter amortization

The following figures refer to a $100,000 mortgage at 10% interest.

Amortization period in years	25 years	20 years	15 years	10 years
Monthly payment of principal and interest	$894.50	$951.70	$1,062.30	$1,310.30
Total mortgage payments made during this period	$268,350	$228,408	$191,214	$157,236

Source: Canadian Bankers Association.

Money Talk

"Start your mortgage with as few years as possible. Everybody just assumed that our first mortgage would be for 25 years, but we really looked at the numbers and decided we could handle the cost of paying it over 20 years instead."
- Jackie, 31, mother of two.

- Reduce your amortization period each time you renew your mortgage. If your income is on the rise, try reducing your amortization period the next time your mortgage comes up for renewal. The fact that you started out with a 25-year amortization period on your mortgage doesn't mean that you have to stick with that particular game plan.

- Increase your payment frequency. You can save an amazing amount of money by paying your mortgage on a weekly or biweekly rather than a monthly basis (see Table 5.8) because you'll actually end up making the equivalent of 13 monthly mortgage payments each year. This also happens to be one of the least painful methods of paying off your mortgage early: you'll hardly even notice that you've made an extra payment.

Table 5.8: Accelerated biweekly vs. monthly payments

The calculations below are based on a $100,000 mortgage at 6.5% interest compounded semi-annually.

Payment frequency	Number of payments	Interest	Principal
Monthly ($670 per month)	300 (25 years)	$100,956	$100,000
Accelerated biweekly ($335 every two weeks)	538 (20 years, 9 months)	$80,354	$100,000
Amount saved		$20,602	

Source: Canadian Bankers Association.

- Take advantage of the prepayment clause in your mortgage. Make additional lump sum payments and/or increase your monthly payments as often as possible.

- When you're renewing your mortgage, resist the temptation to reduce your payment just because mortgage rates have dropped. Instead, decrease your amortization period so that you'll be making roughly the same size of payments.

- Consider refinancing if mortgage rates tumble. Even if you have to pay the equivalent of three months' interest (as is the case with CHMC mortgages), it may be worthwhile to refinance at a lower interest rate. Note: Not all mortgage lenders will allow you to walk away from your mortgage quite this easily. Some may ask you to pay the interest rate differential (IRD)—the difference between what you would have paid under the original terms of the mortgage and what you will pay under the refinanced mortgage—a requirement that eliminates any benefit of refinancing your existing mortgage.

Show Me the Money!

By law, any mortgage in Canada with a term longer than five years automatically becomes open on the fifth anniversary. This means that you can pay off the balance of your mortgage or refinance your mortgage and only be hit with a maximum three-month interest penalty.

Selling your house

If you're planning to sell your home, you'll also want to look for ways to cut costs. Here are a few tips that could save you thousands of dollars:

- If you're intending to use the services of a real estate agent, try to nego-tiate for a reduced commission rate. You're more likely to be successful if you've purchased or sold a home through this agent before or if your house is a high-end property. Many agents are willing to drop the stan-dard 6 percent Multiple Listing Service (MLS) commission down to 5 percent on homes over $200,000 and 4 percent on homes over $400,000.

the Bottom line

While you might think you're going to save yourself a small fortune by selling your house yourself, you could miss out on making a sale altogether. For one thing, you're an amateur when it comes to establishing a selling price for your home; it's easy to scare off potential buyers if you price your property too high. Unfortunately, there's an even greater problem: as a private vendor, you won't be able to list the home in the Multiple Listing Service (MLS)—the very place that most potential buyers turn for leads on properties for sale.

- Look for a real estate agent who can advise you how to make your house more marketable. It may be worth your while to invest the time and money into repainting your house, but it might not be worthwhile to go crazy with other types of home decorating projects (see Table 5.9 for details).

Table 5.9: The Appraisal Institute of Canada's top ten renovation projects to increase the value of your home

1. Kitchen
2. Bathroom
3. Interior painting
4. Finished basement
5. Exterior painting
6. Addition of a main-floor family room
7. New furnace or heating system
8. Landscaping
9. Addition of a separate living unit
10. Energy efficient features

Source: Jim Carroll and Rick Broadhead, *Canadian Money Management Online.*

As you can see, there's a lot to consider when you're thinking about buying or selling a home. Now that you're armed with the facts, you'll be able to make the best possible real estate moves for your family.

Six

Hello Minivan, Goodbye Car

There's no denying it: owning and operating a vehicle is an expensive proposition. Even if you manage to squeeze your growing family into the most budget-friendly, fuel-efficient subcompact car you can find, that car's still going to cost you a couple of hundred dollars per month to run. And if you succumb to peer pressure and end up purchasing a minivan (the modern-day equivalent of the 1975 wood-panelled station wagon), you could find yourself spending considerably more of your after-tax dollars on automotive expenditures.

In this chapter, we'll talk about what it really costs to own and operate a new car, how to save money when you're purchasing a new or used vehicle, how to save money on your financing costs if you require a car loan, and what you can do to reduce the amount of money you spend on automobile insurance.

The Money Pit Revisited

Think your house is a money pit? Think again. The biggest money pit in your life is likely to be that two-ton hunk of steel that's parked out on your driveway.

While there's no denying that there are pleasures associated with car ownership—that new-car smell can be practically intoxicating—there is also a considerable amount of pain. Cars are like demanding lovers that take, take, take, and then break your heart. They're expensive to feed. They can be temperamental. And they have a knack for letting you down when you need them most.

The car-worshipping crowd aside, most Canadians view car ownership as a necessary evil. Unless you're fortunate enough to live on a bus route or near a government-subsidized commuter train, you may have no choice but to make the commitment to own and operate a car.

And what a commitment it is! According to the most recent figures from the Canadian Automobile Association, car ownership doesn't come cheap:

- The average cost of owning and operating a car in Canada in 1998 was $7,601.
- It cost $131 more to operate a vehicle in Canada in 1998 than it did in 1997—a 1.8 percent increase. Table 6.1 shows the relative costs by province.

Table 6.1: The most expensive provinces in which to operate a car

1. Ontario
2. Quebec
3. Newfoundland
4. Nova Scotia
5. New Brunswick
6. Prince Edward Island
7. British Columbia
8. Alberta
9. Yukon/Northwest Territories
10. Saskatchewan
11. Manitoba

Source: Canadian Automobile Association 1999 survey of driving costs.

- The average cost per kilometer for fuel, oil, maintenance, and tires for a car with a driving distance of 18,000 km was 9.7 cents per kilometer.

As you can see, keeping a car on the road can demand a significant chunk of your family's take-home pay. That's why it's important to look for ways to keep your car expenditures as low as possible—a process that should begin the moment you start shopping for a car.

How to get the best possible price on a new or used car

New or used. Used or new. You've probably mulled the two options around in your head long enough to give yourself a headache. If you buy a new car, you're less likely to end up being stranded on some remote rural road with a baby and a toddler in the car. On the other hand, if you buy a used car, you just might be able to afford to buy groceries from time to time.

Regardless of which route you decide to go, you'll want to do whatever you can to bring the purchase price down as low as possible. Here are a few tips on getting the best possible deal on a new or used car.

- **Do your homework.** Find out what the vehicle you're considering is selling for elsewhere by checking out other dealers in your area and by visiting the Web sites of the growing number of companies who are in the business of selling vehicles online. That way, you'll have plenty of ammunition when you start talking to the salesperson at your local car dealership.

- **Get your financing in place.** If you walk into a car dealership armed with a preapproved car loan, you're sending out a strong signal to the sales staff that you're a serious buyer who's ready to make a deal. That may encourage them to give you their best deal right off the bat rather than putting you through the usual car negotiation torture test.

- **Ignore the sticker price.** In most cases, you should be able to bring down the sticker price on a moderately-priced vehicle by at least a few hundred dollars—and sometimes even more. The car-buying gurus suggest that you ask to see a copy of the invoice that the dealer received from the manufacturer, since it more accurately indicates what the dealership actually paid for the car. If the dealer seems reluctant to chop the price, ask for freebies instead. See if you can convince him or her to throw in a set of car mats, a year's worth of oil changes, and other items that you'd end up paying for out of your own pocket anyway.

- **Make sure you're comparing apples to apples.** If you're comparison shopping between various makes and models, it's not enough simply to compare sticker prices. You also have to consider such factors as what it costs to maintain each type of vehicle, how expensive parts are, and what you can expect to pay for insurance. Don't just take the manufacturer or car dealer's word about the operating costs, however. Make a point of talking to other people who are in the know: friends and family members who own this particular type of car, the mechanic at your local garage, the friendly fellow in the automotive department at your local automotive store, and so on.

the Bottom line

Before you buy a car of a particular make and model, make a pit stop at your local automotive supply store and find out what you're going to end up paying for oil filters, brake pads, and other frequently replaced parts. Certain makes and models of cars can be extremely expensive to keep on the road. Make sure you know this up front.

- **Time your purchase carefully.** You can save significant amounts of money if you buy your new car on a day when the salesperson you're dealing with is most motivated to make a sale. According to Corey Sandler, author of *The Secrets of the Savvy Consumer,* one of the best days to shop for a new car is December 31—especially if it's snowing! "First of all," he explains, "this is an especially quiet time because of the holiday period. The snowstorm helps cut down on visitors, too. Finally, dealerships routinely create sales contests and quotas, and they are almost always tied to the end of the week, the end of the month, or the end of the year." A salesperson who is just one car sale away from landing a big bonus as part of an in-house sales promotion will practically be willing to gift wrap the car for you if it means you'll actually take it!

- **Feign a total lack of interest.** You lose a lot of your negotiating ability the moment the salesperson discovers that you've fallen in love with a particular vehicle. That's why it's important to play it cool, even if you know that the minivan you just test drove is definitely the one you want. You're going to be able to negotiate a far better price if you let the salesperson know that you are bored by the process of shopping for a car and that you couldn't care less about all of the jazzy features that he's determined to tell you about. You will have played your cards right if you manage to give an Academy Award performance that leaves the salesperson with the impression that you're prepared to walk if you can't get the price that you want.

Facts and Figures

Don't expect to get the same loan rate on a used car as you would on a new car. A loan on a used car typically costs two to three percent more than a loan on a brand new car.

- **Don't overdose on options.** While options like sun roofs, power windows, and remote keyless entries are nice to have, they are by no means essential. Before you agree to spend an extra $5,000 to pay for the option package that entitles you to all these flashy extras, stop to consider what else you might be able to do with that $5,000 you're itching to spend—like paying down your mortgage or making a hefty contribution to your RRSP. And if you're planning to borrow that $5,000, take a moment to consider what you'll actually pay over the life of the loan. Once you put down your calculator, you'll probably decide that rolling down your own window really isn't that much of a hardship after all!

- **Forget about trying to keep up with the Joneses.** Don't rush out to buy a minivan just because the family across the street has one. Stop to consider whether you actually need a vehicle this size. Remember: it costs a lot more money to own and operate a full-sized minivan than it does to keep a subcompact sedan on the road.

- **Pass on the chance to have the dealer undercoat, rustproof, pinstripe, or otherwise mess with the new vehicle.** You'll simply be adding to the purchase price. (Note: If you've got your heart set on having any of these services performed, plan to go elsewhere after you've bought the car.)

- **Consider your family's long-term needs.** If you've got three children and you intend to have another baby in the next year or two, there's no point buying a five-person sedan. You would simply have to trade it in—and probably take a painful financial hit as well—when the new baby arrives. This is not to say that you can always anticipate all of your family's needs in advance: surprises can and do occur. If the stork leaves an unexpected bundle of joy on your porch, you'd just better hope that he drops off the keys to a new minivan, too!

- **Just say no to credit.** It's almost always a bad idea to borrow money for items like cars that depreciate in value over time, and most new cars depreciate a minimum of 20 to 30 percent within their first year. While you might have no choice but to borrow the money if you've got your heart set on a new car—after all, not very many families with young children have an extra $20,000 or so sitting in the bank!—you might be able to swing a cash deal (or, at the very least, borrow less money) if you changed your buying strategy and decided to shop around for a second-hand vehicle instead.

- **If you're buying a used car, have it inspected by a mechanic you trust.** The $50 or so that you pay for a quick checkup could save you thousands of dollars if it turns out that there's something seriously wrong with the vehicle.

Winning at the trade-in game

Buying a car is complicated enough. Buying a new car and trading in your old one at the same time is even more challenging. Here's what to do to ensure that you're receiving top dollar for your vehicle.

- Invest some money in your vehicle before you trade it in. The money you spend on a tune-up and a bumper-to-bumper cleaning could increase the value of your car by as much as a thousand dollars, especially if there are a lot of stains in your car's interior.

- If you're negotiating a deal with a car dealership, be sure to play your trade-in card very carefully. Automobile dealers are notorious for trying to pull a fast one on you when you're trying to trade in one car and purchase another. They like to blur the two transactions together so that you focus on the balance owing rather than what you're getting for your old car and paying for your new one. That's why it's generally a good idea to keep the fact that you have a car to trade in a secret until you have managed to negotiate the best possible deal on the new vehicle.

- If you're not happy with the pittance that the dealership offers you for your old vehicle—an all-too-likely scenario, I'm afraid—then be prepared to go into the automotive sales business yourself. Run a classified advertisement in your local newspaper or in a publication such as the *Auto Trader* and wait for your phone to start ringing. (Note: Your phone is more likely to start ringing if you price your car appropriately. Do some research so that you'll have a realistic idea about what other cars of the same make, age, and condition are selling for, and then price your vehicle accordingly.)

Saving money on a car loan

While the best way to buy a car is by paying cash, that isn't always possible. If you're going to be borrowing money to pay for a vehicle, be sure to line up the best financing deal possible. Here are a few tips:

- Tell the dealership to keep its money. Unless you are able to take advantage of one of those super-duper deals on dealer financing, it's generally not worth your while to obtain financing from the dealership. Nine times out of ten, you can get a better deal somewhere other than the dealership. Note: If a particular car dealership is offering what appears to be a truly extraordinary interest rate, be sure to read the fine print: often the interest rate only applies for a short period of time, at which point you start paying a significantly higher interest rate.

- Consider joining a credit union. They tend to offer bargain basement interest rates on car loans—rates that are often a good percentage point or more lower than what you can get through a bank.

- Steer clear of front-end loans. They are a nasty piece of work. Unlike a simple loan, in which the amount of principal you're paying increases and the amount of interest you're paying decreases with each payment, with a front-end loan you pay interest on the original amount borrowed each and every month throughout the entire term of the loan. According to Robert K. Heady, Christy Heady, and Bruce McDougall, authors of *The Complete Idiot's Guide to Managing Your Money in Canada*, the $373 payment that you would expect to pay on a simple loan for $15,000 at 9 percent interest would balloon to $425 per month if you opted for a front-end loan instead.

- Don't get seduced by a low loan payment. While it's tempting to fixate on the amount of money you have to fork over each month, you should be more concerned with what that loan is going to cost you by the time you finish paying for your car.
- Put down as much money as possible and then pay off your car loan as soon as possible. The sooner you pay your car off, the more you will save on interest charges. Note: Before you start doubling up on payments, however, be sure to check with your lender to find out if there are any prepayment penalties or whether it is even possible to save money on interest charges by prepaying the loan early. (Sometimes the lender simply holds these additional payments, rather than applying them to the outstanding principal.)

Show Me the Money!

Think twice before you finance your car purchase with a home equity loan. It's one thing to lose your car if you default on a car payment; it's quite another to lose your house.

The hidden costs of leasing

Leasing a car is a lot like having a car loan, except for one important difference: you're only paying off a portion of the principal with your monthly payments. Consequently, when the lease expires, there is still money owing on the car. At this point, you have to decide whether you would like to purchase the car at the buyout price (the street value of the vehicle at that time, according to the dealer) or give the car back to the dealer and start looking for a new set of wheels.

Leasing makes more sense for some families than for others. If you and your partner are in the habit of trading in your new car for another vehicle every two years or so, you would probably be further ahead by leasing. If, on the other hand, you're quite happy driving around a ten-year-old clunker that's held together with coat hangers and duct tape, then you would definitely get your money's worth out of purchasing a car.

If you do decide to proceed with a lease, it's important to go over the lease agreement with a fine-toothed comb so that you'll be absolutely clear about what you're getting yourself in for. Here are a few questions you'll want to ask before you sign on the dotted line:

- **What is the maximum number of kilometers you're allowed to drive under the terms of the lease?** Make sure it's a realistic figure or you'll be hit with some hefty mileage charges when the lease comes up for renewal.
- **What kind of insurance coverage are you required to carry under the terms of the lease?** Some leases require that you carry extremely comprehensive coverage, something that can add to your insurance costs.
- **What is the definition of "normal wear and tear"?** Are minor scratches a problem or does the dealer understand that it's next to impossible to keep a vehicle in pristine condition when it's being used to lug around a carload of kids on a daily basis?
- **What are your responsibilities with regard to routine maintenance?** Do you need to keep detailed records to demonstrate that the car was properly serviced by a reputable garage?
- **What would happen if you lost your job and you were no longer able to keep up with your payments?** Would you be liable for all remaining payments during the lifetime of the lease?

Here's a painless way to zero in on the automobile insurance companies that are likely to offer you the best rates. The Consumer's Guide to Insurance—a free consumer watchdog service that is not affiliated with any insurance company—will provide you with leads on the three lowest insurance rates on your particular vehicle. You can reach the automated service 24 hours a day by calling 416-686-0531, or you can speak with a live human being by calling 1-888-228-1305.

The do's and don'ts of shopping for auto insurance

Regardless of whether you decide to lease or buy your next vehicle, you're going to have to spend some time shopping for auto insurance. Here are a few tips to help you get the maximum bang for your automobile insurance buck:

Do's

Remember to tell your insurance agent about any special safety and security features that your car has. You may be entitled to a reduction in premiums if your car has security alarms, air bags, antilock brakes, or other similar types of features.

Save yourself some money by choosing the highest possible deductible for both collision (damage to your car that is caused through a collision) and comprehensive (other types of damage to your car) or, if your car is worth next to nothing, not bothering to carry these types of coverage at all.

Consider carrying uninsured or underinsured motorist liability coverage, even if you've got medical and disability insurance through your employer or a private plan. This type of coverage, which allows you to collect for lost wages, medical expenses, and any pain and suffering you experienced as a result of an automobile accident with an uninsured or underinsured motorist, also applies to passengers in your car who might not otherwise have adequate medical and disability coverage.

Don'ts

Don't try to save money in the wrong places. You could end up with bigger money problems than you can even imagine if you aren't carrying adequate amounts of bodily injury/property damage liability. Rather than playing insurance roulette and gambling that you won't get sued, ensure that you have enough liability insurance to protect all of the assets you've worked so hard to accumulate. Some financial planners recommend that you carry an amount equivalent to anywhere from two to five times the total value of your assets, but even that may be a little low. Remember, you don't just stand to lose everything you've managed to accumulate to date: your future earnings could also be garnisheed in the event that you're on the losing end of a lawsuit.

Operating costs revisited

Looking for some ways to reduce the amount of money that you spend on owning and operating a vehicle? Here are a few commonsense tips that could put significant amounts of cash back in your wallet:

Show Me the Money!

Here's a quick way to estimate the annual depreciation costs on your vehicle. Take the original purchase price and subtract the estimated trade-in value at the time you plan to dispose of the car. (The classified ads are a great source of this type of information.) Then divide this figure by the number of years you own and operate the vehicle. Voila! You've got an annual depreciation figure to work with.

- **Use your car less often.** The fact that you own the darned thing doesn't necessarily mean you have to use it each and every time you leave the house. Take your kids for a walk or a bike ride when it's time to mail a letter at the post office or fill a prescription at the drugstore. It's a great way to save money, get fit, and have fun at the same time.

- **Carpool to work.** If you only drive your car every other day, you'll cut your commuting costs in half. You'll also only have to cope with rush-hour traffic half as often—reason enough to find someone else in your neighbourhood who's willing to split the driving. If you can't find anyone to carpool with, consider using public transit every other day instead. Note: If you do decide to carpool, make sure your insurance is adequate.

- **Pass on the designer gasoline.** Pull into any gas station and you're likely to be faced with at least three choices at the pump: ho-hum gas, good gas, and super-terrific gas. According to Eric Tyson and Tony Martin, authors of *Personal Finance for Dummies for Canadians*, premium gasolines are highly overrated and don't justify the added expense. Just stick with regular gas (or whatever fancy name the gas station you're using has chosen to describe its ordinary, everyday gas).

- **Maintain your car properly.** Remember that an ounce of prevention is worth a pound of cure. It's a lot cheaper to maintain your car properly than it is to pay for problems that arise due to poor maintenance. What's more, you'll feel a lot more confident that your car is going to make it from Point A to Point B without any help from the CAA—reason enough to keep your car well maintained.

Seven

HITTING THE BOOKS

While it may seem a little crazy to be worrying about Junior's university tuition before he's even passed Crawling 101, there's something to be said about setting up an educational savings plan while he's still very young. It all has to do with the magic of compound interest: the more time your money has to grow, the more money there will be to pay for your child's education when the time comes.

Despite what many people believe, you don't have to put away huge sums of money each year to achieve your goal of paying for your child's education. If you put $2,000 per year into an RESP and manage to average 8 percent growth per year on your investment from the time your baby is born until she reaches age 18, you will have built up $75,000 by the time your budding genius is ready to head off to Harvard.

Money Talk

"The [Canadian Federation of Students] estimates that the cost of a four-year undergraduate arts degree, including living expenses, will rise from about $40,000 today to $67,000 by the time children born this year reach age 18. The Bank of Montreal puts the future cost at about $75,000, based in part on an assumption that tuition fees will continue to rise faster than the rate of inflation, as they have so far this decade."
Source: John Schofield, "College on the Layaway," *Maclean's Guide to Personal Finance 1999*.

The challenge, of course, is finding the $40 a week you're going to have to set aside if you're serious about achieving that goal. That, for most families, is the most difficult part. While most parents are committed to the idea of helping to finance their children's education, very few actually manage to set aside funds on a regular basis. A 1996 Angus Reid Group study that involved more than 1,000 Canadian parents showed that while 77 percent of parents see the value of saving for their children's education, only 24 percent of them actually manage to do so. The researchers found that educational savings ranked third in the typical family's financial priorities, right after paying off the mortgage and contributing to an RRSP.

Table 7.1: The most and least expensive provinces in which to attend university in 1998

Newfoundland	$12,374
Prince Edward Island	10,507
Nova Scotia	10,139
Ontario	9,886
Manitoba	8,186
Saskatchewan	7,789
Alberta	8,709
British Columbia	8,645
New Brunswick	7,960
Quebec	7,185

Source: Gordon Pape and Frank Jones, *Head Start: How to Save for Your Children's or Grandchildren's Education.*

Why Junior needs your help

Even if you managed to pay your own way through university, it's unlikely that your child is going to be able to follow in your footsteps. The costs of tuition and other education-related expenses have increased at a rate far greater than the rate of inflation. Bottom line? No matter how bright or hardworking your child turns out to be, he's likely to need at least a little help from you in financing his education. Here's why:

• Tuition fees have more than doubled since the early 1980s and they're expected to continue to rise in years to come (see Table 7.2).

Table 7.2: The rising cost of university tuition

Year entering university	Estimated cost of four-year program (with residence costs)	Estimated cost of four-year program (without residence costs)
2003–04	$68,700	$40,600
2004–05	73,300	43,600
2005–06	78,100	46,800
2006–07	83,300	50,300
2007–08	88,800	54,000
2008–09	94,600	58,000
2009–10	100,900	62,300
2010–11	107,500	66,900
2011–12	114,600	71,800
2012–13	122,200	77,100
2013–14	130,300	82,800
2014–15	138,900	89,000
2015–16	148,000	95,600

Source: USC Education Savings Plans, cited in Gordon Pape and Frank Jones, *Head Start: How to Save for Your Children's or Grandchildren's Education*.

- Government support for universities dropped by 14.1 percent between 1992 and 1996, and tuition fees have soared by an average annual rate of 11 percent throughout the 1990s, up from a 6.5 percent rate in the 1980s.

- According to *Maclean's*, university tuition fee increases for the 1998–99 academic year ranged from a low of 0.7 percent in British Columbia (where tuition costs average $2,736 per year) to a high of 9.2 percent in Ontario (where tuition costs average $3,564 per year).

- It's almost impossible to earn enough income through part-time and summer employment to finance a post-secondary education. This explains why, in 1998, more than half of students enrolled in post-secondary programs turned to the Canada Student Loan Program for assistance.

- The amount of debt that students are carrying has increased dramatically in recent years. According to Statistics Canada, the average amount owed by a post-secondary graduate in 1998 was $25,000—a whopping increase over the $17,000 that the average graduate owed in 1995.

How soon to start saving for your child's education

You may find that you are hit with so many baby-related expenses during your child's first year of life that it's almost impossible to scrape together the funds you need to start saving for her education. Rather than getting discouraging and giving up entirely, you should simply set aside whatever funds you can and make an effort to increase the size and frequency of your contributions as your family's bottom line allows.

You might decide, for example, to invest all or a part of the Child Tax Benefit payment you receive from the federal government each month. (Note: if your family income is exceptionally high, you might not qualify for this particular benefit at all. See Chapter 11 on tax breaks for details.) The great thing about investing the Child Tax Benefit is that it is money that "belongs" to your child—at least in the eyes of Revenue Canada. This means that the normal income attribution rules don't apply: if your child earns interest on this money, the interest income will be considered to be his, not yours, so you won't have to declare it on your tax return. There's just one drawback to relying exclusively on the Child Tax Benefit to save for your child's education: if it's substantial enough to be worth investing, chances are you need the money to pay for your child's day-to-day needs such as food and clothing!

Show Me the Money!

Don't mix your child's income with general family funds if you want any interest it earns to belong to your child in the eyes of Revenue Canada.

Other potential sources of funds for educational savings include gifts from relatives and any employment income your child earns over the years. Once again, it's important to keep these funds separate from your general family funds so that you won't find yourself having to declare the tax on any interest your child earns on her money.

Note: Gifts to your child, whether from yourself or another relative, have to be "irrevocably given" if you're going to beat the tax collector. Revenue Canada doesn't look kindly on arrangements in which parents and grandparents "give" money to a child in order to avoid declaring tax on the income, but then don't actually want to hand over control of that money to the child, perhaps out of fear that the child will want to use "his" money to buy a motorcycle the day he turns 16 (something you can only get around by putting the funds in a Registered Education Savings Plan). Bottom line? It's either a gift or it's not. You can't have it both ways.

You can get the scoop on tax attribution rules, trusts, and other related issues in Frank Jones and Gordon Pape's book *Head Start: How to Save for Your Children's or Grandchildren's Education* (Stoddart, 1998).

Show Me the Money!

Income that your child receives as a direct beneficiary of a will is considered to be his or her own in the eyes of Revenue Canada.

The good news department

A couple of years ago, this chapter would have been all doom-and-gloom. Registered education savings plans (RESPs) were a less-than-attractive savings vehicle for families. You could dutifully contribute a certain amount of money each month for 18 months, only to lose all the accumulated interest if Jennifer or Jason decided to embark on a career with the local fast food joint rather than hitting the books at college or university. Many families lost thousands of dollars of accumulated interest as a result.

While there are still a few drawbacks to post-1998 RESPs (we'll get into that in a minute), they are a whole lot better than anything that has been available up until now. For one thing, the federal government kicks in a 20 percent Canada Education Savings grant (CESG) on the first $2,000 of annual contributions for each child. That's like getting a 20 percent return on your investment right away. Then there's the fact that the government has changed the RESP rules to reduce the financial risks that families face by using this particular savings vehicle—the nightmarish scenario that we described above.

Let's take a look at the fine print on RESPs.

What is a registered educational savings plan?

As the name implies, a registered education savings plan (RESP) is an education savings plan that has been registered with Revenue Canada. Even though its name sounds a lot like "registered retirement savings plan," the two work in totally different ways. While your RRSP contribution is tax deductible, your RESP contribution isn't. There are, however, tax advantages to contributing to an RESP: the interest that accumulates within the plan is tax-sheltered until it is withdrawn, at which point it is taxed in the hands of the recipient, not the contributor.

the Bottom line

An RESP does not have to be divided up in the event of separation or divorce. You and your former spouse can continue to hold the plan jointly.

The maximum annual contribution to an RESP is $4,000 per beneficiary and there is a $42,000 lifetime contribution limit per beneficiary. Unused RESP contribution room cannot be carried forward (as is the case with RRSPs), so this is definitely a case of "use it or lose it."

An RESP plan automatically matures 25 years after it is set up, whether your child has actually started post-secondary studies or not. If all of the beneficiaries of the plan were 21 years of age or older and you realized that there was no longer any hope of any of them continuing their studies at the post-secondary level, you would be allowed to fold the plan early.

What's the difference between an individual RESP plan and a RESP group plan?

An individual RESP gives you the freedom to make your own investment decisions. You decide how you're going to invest the funds within your plan and you can change your contribution levels at any time.

A pooled RESP is a plan that you hold in common with other investors. The fund manager makes the decisions for you. These plans tend to be more restrictive than individual RESPs in the event that your child chooses not to pursue a post-secondary education, so be sure to read the fine print before you sign on the dotted line.

Who can contribute to an RESP?

Anyone can contribute to a child's RESP provided that the annual contribution limit of $4,000 and the lifetime contribution limit of $42,000 haven't been reached. Potential contributors will have to obtain your child's social insurance number from you before they will be able to set up a separate plan for your child or contribute to her existing RESP plan.

If a well-meaning relative suggests that you set up more than one RESP to get around the contribution limits, don't bother. Those folks at Revenue Canada are smart. You could run up a fairly hefty overcontribution penalty (one percent per month) if the total amount contributed was to exceed $4,000 per year. Even worse, if you pulled out the amount that you overcontributed, those funds would still count against your child's annual and lifetime contribution levels. (Now that's nasty!)

Where does the Canada Education Savings Grant fit in?

The Canada Education Savings Grant was introduced in the 1998 federal budget. It provides a 20 percent government-paid subsidy to your own RESP contributions, up to a maximum of $400 per child per year or $7,200 over an 18-year period. (The plan itself can be kept open for up to 25 years.) You don't have to fill out any paperwork to get the grant: the plan administrator handles this for you. You just sit back and watch the grant grow—and grow it will. Just think about it: if your RESP managed to earn an 8 percent annual rate of return and you were eligible for the maximum grant each year, your RESP could be $15,000 bigger than it might otherwise have been, thanks to your friends in Ottawa.

Show Me the Money!

Don't expect to get a Canada Education Savings Grant if you don't get around to setting up an RESP until your child is in the last year or two of high school. A grant will be paid when your child is age 16 and 17 only if you contributed at least $300 per year for a minimum of four years before your child turned 16 or if contributions you made prior to that time totalled at least $4,000. This is obviously the federal government's way of preventing parents from trying for a last-minute grant grab.

If you find it difficult to make your maximum contribution when you're simultaneously purchasing car seats, cribs, strollers, and other baby paraphernalia, don't torture yourself by thinking about the Canada Education Savings Grant that you otherwise might have had. You still might be able to obtain the grant to which your child is entitled by increasing your contributions in future years. Obviously, there are limits to how much you can contribute to an RESP in any given year ($4,000), and your RESP contributions themselves these can't be carried forward, so you'll have to be careful not to get too far behind in your contributions.

Let's consider how this might play out in real life. You can contribute a maximum of $4,000 to an RESP each year, but only $2,000 of that money is eligible for a Canada Education Savings Grant. If you managed to squirrel away only $500 during your baby's first year of life, you would get a grant of $100. You could, however, make a $3,500 contribution the following year, still be under the $4,000 contribution maximum, and obtain a $700 Canada Education Savings Grant (the current year's $400 maximum plus the $300 in unused grants from the previous year).

When and how can your child access the money in the plan?

Your child can start to access funds in his RESP once he starts attending a qualifying program at an eligible post-secondary institution. The funds that are removed from the plan in order to cover his education-related expenses (tuition, books, equipment, lab fees, student fees, transportation costs, accommodation fees) are known as educational assistance payments (EAP).

In order to qualify for these payments your child must either be

- enrolled as a full-time student in a qualifying education program at a post-secondary educational institution (either by attending classes in person or by taking courses through distance education) or
- enrolled on a less-than-full-time basis due to a mental or physical impairment that prevents her from attending school full-time (a medical certificate is required)

A qualifying educational program is a post-secondary program that

- is offered by a foreign or Canadian university, college, or other qualifying educational institution that offers post-secondary courses
- lasts three consecutive weeks or more (if it is offered by an educational institution within Canada) or thirteen weeks or more (if it is offered by an educational institution outside of Canada)
- requires students to spend ten or more hours per week attending classes and/or doing their course work

the Bottom line

According to Gordon Pape and Frank Jones, authors of *Head Start: How to Save for Your Children's and Grandchildren's Education,* it's important to read the fine print on your RESP agreement before you sign on the dotted line. They warn that some RESP companies have much stricter rules about which types of educational institutions your child must attend in order to obtain educational assistance payments. In other words, the government could say yay, but the people who are holding your money could say nay!

How and when are the educational assistance payments made?

A student cannot receive more that $5,000 in educational assistance payments until he has completed 13 consecutive weeks in a qualifying educational program. Assuming that the student continues to qualify to receive such payments after the thirteenth week, he is then able to withdraw as much or as little money as he needs to cover his education-related expenses from the plan. (Just a reminder: Education-related expenses are more than just tuition. They also include books, student fees, transportation costs, accommodation costs, and so on.)

If the $5,000 educational assistance payment isn't sufficient to cover a student's educational expenses during the first 13 weeks of her program (possibly because the cost of tuition for a particular program is substantially higher than what you would normally expect to pay, as is the case with certain professional programs), the student may ask to have the Minister of Human Resources Development approve a larger educational assistance payment. While this sounds tremendously complicated, you simply write a letter to your RESP company explaining your child's circumstances and the company seeks government approval on your behalf.

Show Me the Money!

Your child will not be eligible for educational assistance payments if she is working full-time or if the program that she is taking is part of her employment.

What happens if your child decides not to go to college or university?

Now we get to the scary part: what happens if you've done your bit to build up a nice little nest egg for Junior, but he decides that he'd like to flip hamburgers instead?

As much as you might hate to even consider the possibility that your child might not even need the money that you're working so hard to save on her behalf, not every child wants to pursue a post-secondary education. That's why it's important for you to understand up front what would happen to the money in your child's RESP if she decided to pass on the opportunity to go to college or university.

If you have more than one child, the easiest thing to do is to designate his brother or sister as the beneficiary of the plan instead. If that's not possible, you'll have no choice but to fold the plan.

Getting back the money that you've contributed to the RESP over the years is easy. You are allowed to make tax-free withdrawals of the capital that you contributed to the plan at any time. It's getting the rest of the money out of the plan that's a whole lot more complicated. The first thing that will happen is that the federal government will snatch back all the Canadian Education Savings Grant money that it contributed to your child's plan over the years. They don't just take the grant, of course, but also any interest that it has accumulated over the years.

That's the bad news. Fortunately, there's also some good news. Thanks to those far-reaching changes that were introduced in the 1998 federal budget, in most cases, you will no longer have to walk away from the interest on the capital that you contributed to your child's RESP. You can choose to transfer as much as $50,000 of these accumulated earnings (per child) into your own RRSP and incur no tax penalty at all. (Obviously, you need to have the necessary RRSP contribution room in order to go this route.)

If, however, you don't choose to or aren't able to roll the money into your RRSP, things get kind of ugly. The proceeds of the plan are treated as personal income and taxed in your hands. In addition to taking the usual tax hit, you are also required to pay a 20 percent penalty. According to authors Gordon Pape and Frank Jones, this pushes the tax rate up to an eye-popping 65 to 75 percent in most cases!

Money Talk

Heidi, a 23-year-old single mother of one, starting saving for her son's post-secondary education shortly after he was born. "It's a huge priority of mine to be able to put my child through university or to send him to some other type of post-secondary educational institution. Each month, I am putting away a little extra for his future."

You can reduce the tax hit a little by either splitting the funds with your partner (something that is only possible if you were co-contributors to the plan right from the very beginning) or taking the money over in two installments that span two tax years, but that's about the best deal you're going to be able to cut for yourself. Once an accumulated income payment (any withdrawal of contributions that is neither a refund of the money you contributed or an educational assistance payment) is made from an RESP, the clock starts ticking and you only have until the end of February of the following year to close the plan entirely.

As with anything else involving Revenue Canada, there's some additional fine print that you need to know about. In order to take advantage of either of the two alternatives outlined above (transferring the RESP funds into an RRSP or taking an accumulated income payment in cash), the plan must have been in existence for at least ten years, all beneficiaries must be at least 21

Table 7.3: Estimating U.S. Tuition costs

Thinking of sending your child to a U.S. college or university? Here's how to calculate what that stateside education could cost you. According to Family Money magazine, the average cost of a four-year public university education (tuition only) is $8,000 U.S. per year. At a private college, it's $20,000 U.S. and at the most prestigious universities—the Harvards, Yales, and Stanfords— it's $28,000 U.S. per year. To figure out what a four-year undergraduate degree could cost by the time your child is ready to enroll in college or university, simply multiply the tuition-only figure above by the college cost multiplier listed below.

Year	Multiplier
1998	4.31
1999	4.53
2000	4.76
2001	5.00
2002	5.25
2003	5.51
2004	5.78
2005	6.07
2006	6.37
2007	6.69
2008	7.03
2009	7.38
2010	7.75
2011	8.13
2012	8.53
2013	8.96
2014	9.41
2015	9.88
2016	10.38
2017	10.90
2018	11.44
2019	12.02
2020	12.62
2021	13.25

Note: Based on five percent annual increases.

Source: *Family Money.*

years of age and not pursuing post-secondary studies, and you must be a resident of Canada. If any of these conditions aren't met, the income that has accumulated in the plan over the years will be forfeited. (Actually, the federal government will "allow" you to donate them to the post-secondary institution of your choice! Talk about a shotgun charitable donation!)

As you can see, while RESPs are a whole lot better than they used to be, they can still end up costing you a fortune in lost income if your child decides not to pursue a post-secondary education. Fortunately, at least one study has shown that children are more likely to head to college or university if the funds for their education are available.

The key to coming up with the money you will need to underwrite Junior's education is, of course, to start contributing early so that your money will have the maximum length of time to grow. Who knows? If you play your cards right, maybe Junior will even remember to thank you in her speech when she's chosen as class valedictorian!

Eight

SURVIVING THE FIRST YEAR

There's no denying it. Starting a family is expensive. There are so many different demands on your paycheque that you may find yourself wondering how you're ever going to be able to afford to buy everything that Junior needs.

Here's a bit of good news if you've started to panic about whether you are, in fact, financially ready to become a parent. Despite what the salesperson on the floor of the high-priced baby boutique would have you believe, that bundle of joy doesn't have to cost you a bundle—not if you're smart about it.

"So many parents fall into the 'cute and new trap'," says Laura, a 22-year-old mother of one. "Secondhand is just as good as new since babies grow out of things—including equipment—so quickly that items often are barely used."

Babies also don't need nearly as much stuff as we think they do, adds Fiona, a 32-year-old mother of six. "Getting down to the basics of a baby's world, all the baby really needs is his mother: her arms to hold and comfort him, her breasts to nourish him, and her presence to teach him love, security, and trust."

Babies are big business for baby equipment manufacturers. The U.S. juvenile products industry racks up $3.7 billion in sales each year. Canadian parents spend somewhere in the neighbourhood of $370 million each year.

Don't shop till you drop

Take a walk through the baby department of any major retail store and you'll be stunned by the sheer variety of products that are being pitched to parents. In addition to cribs, change tables, strollers, car seats, playpens, baby swings, and all the other big ticket items, you'll find hundreds of other items vying for your attention and a share of your baby equipment budget. Some of them are definitely worth picking up, like those quilted pads that help prevent your baby's head from flopping sideways when she's in her car seat. Then there are those products that you and your baby can definitely live without—like baby-wipe warmers!

Show Me the Money!

Form a purchasing co-op with other members of your childbirth class and use your combined buying power to approach local retailers to negotiate the best possible deal on cribs, car seats, strollers, and so on.

The trick, of course, is to figure out what you need—and what you don't need—before you've worn the numbers off your credit card. Here's a crash course in Baby Equipment 101 for parents-to-be who are looking for ways to avoid overspending when they're shopping for baby.

- Don't shop too early. Shopping for baby should be a third trimester activity, not something you start doing the moment the pregnancy test comes back positive! The more time you spend shopping, the more you're going to spend.

- Don't overlook the fact that you're going to receive an extraordinary number of baby gifts. Even casual acquaintances—neighbours you've only spoken to once and relatives you haven't heard from in years—will show up on your doorstep bearing parcels full of wonderful things. (There's a method in their madness, of course. They know that if they show up with a gift in hand, you'll feel obligated to let them gawk at the new arrival.) If you stick to buying just the essentials before baby arrives, you won't be faced with returning all kinds of items that you don't really need—or watching your best friend's face drop when she discovers that you already have a baby mobile.

Money Talk

"You don't have to carry a diaper bag with Mickey on it. Any bag or knapsack will do. Just get a diaper pad, some diapers, and you're off!"
— Anne, 40, mother of three.

- Don't overbuy. Despite what some of the baby stores would have you believe, all your baby really needs during his first weeks of life are a car seat, a safe place to sleep (a crib, cradle, bassinet, for example); a baby carrier (a sling or a Snugli, for example), some baby clothes, and some diapers. If you've got some extra money in your budget, you might also want to pick up a few extra bells and whistles: a stroller, a baby swing, a baby monitor, and a rocking chair for you and baby to enjoy. These last few items aren't essentials, but they're certainly nice to have.

- Don't clutter your baby's room with furniture that isn't necessary. A dresser is nice to have, but it certainly isn't necessary. You might choose to store your baby's clothes in an oversized Rubbermaid container and store it under your baby's bed. The same goes with the change table: you might find it easier to change a wiggly baby by tossing a waterproof pad on your own bed than by trying to keep her from doing backflips off a tiny wooden platform!

- Watch out for items that pretend to be essentials, but that are anything but. Does it make sense to buy a high-priced garbage can for your child's room, just because it matches his wallpaper?

- Test drive items whenever possible. Before you spend $90 on an Exersaucer (an amazing contraption that allows baby to play in an upright position as soon as she can support her head) or a Jolly Jumper (that ever-popular baby contraption that turns your wriggling six-month-old into a human yo-yo), make sure that your baby is actually going to use it. Babies have distinct preferences from a very young age. Some want nothing more than to be tucked into a Snugli and strapped to your chest; others view it as the baby world equivalent of a straitjacket. Before you fork over the big bucks for any of these items, see if you can borrow a friend's to see if it meets with your baby's approval. (Who knows: maybe the friend might even loan you the item!)

Show Me the Money!

If your coworkers are planning to buy you a baby gift and they ask you what you need, suggest that they pool their funds and buy you something practical like a car seat or a stroller.

- Purchase the base model of a product rather than a more expensive model with features that you may never need. A crib with a double drop railing is about $75 more expensive than one with a single drop railing, for example.

- Check out the cost and availability of replacement parts for strollers and other types of baby equipment before you decide which brand to purchase. Some brands are extremely expensive to repair—assuming replacement parts are available at all.

Your baby's wardrobe

You can spend as much or as little as you'd like on your baby's wardrobe. How much you decide to spend will be determined by how often you're prepared to do laundry and how important it is to you that your baby has a closet full of brand-name garments. (Your baby couldn't care less what he's wearing as long as it's warm, dry, and free of itchy lace and scratchy tags.)

Table 8.1: The Canadian baby layette

You should plan to have these items on hand before your baby arrives. The following chart indicates how much you can expect to spend if you're purchasing each of these items new. If you plan to borrow certain items from friends and relatives or to pick some of them up second-hand, you can expect to spend significantly less.

12 newborn nighties @ $8 each	$96
3 sleepers @ $15 each	45
2 baby towel-and-washcloth sets @ $15 each	30
3 sets of fitted crib sheets @ $10 each	30
12 extra-large receiving blankets @ $5 each	60
3 pairs of socks @ $2 each	6
1 sweater (depending on the season)	15
2 cotton hats @ $10 each	20
1 snowsuit or bunting bag (depending on the season)	40
4 large bibs	30
Total	$372

Source: Adapted from Ann Douglas and John R. Sussman, M.D., *The Unofficial Guide to Having a Baby.*

- Buy only what you need. Babies need clothes, but they don't need dozens of outfits. If you're prepared to do laundry every day or every other day, you should be able to get away with having six outfits in the smaller sizes—perhaps even fewer if baby isn't prone to leaky diapers. Note: If you're expecting twins, you will need approximately one-and-a-half times as much clothing rather than twice as much clothing as you would need if you were having one baby.

- Don't buy too many outfits in the newborn size, but do plan to have at least one outfit in this size on hand: more than one mom's been sure that she was carrying an 11-pound baby, only to watch a six pounder make her grand entrance!
- Don't even think about buying a sleeper that doesn't have crotch snaps. It'll be such a pain to use that you'll never want to be bothered putting it on your baby. (Why there are sleepers like this in the first place is one of life's greatest mysteries.)
- Look for sleepers that are designed to grow with your baby, like the Snugabye brand that have adjustable ankle cuffs.
- Consider using cloth diapers or non-brand-name disposables. While cloth diapers are the environmentally friendly alternative, they aren't for everyone, so if you do decide to go with disposables, try a few generic brands. If you find that they don't work as well as Huggies or Pampers—the two biggest brands here in Canada—then you might want to use the expensive diapers at night when you want your baby to stay dry (and asleep!) as long as possible, and the less expensive generic brands during the day when it's not such a hassle to change a diaper every couple of hours.
- Rather than stocking up on baby wipes, try making your own by filling a squirt bottle with a mixture of liquid baby soap and water and then spraying the liquid on some inexpensive washcloths. If you've absolutely got your heart set on using the disposable baby wipes, make them go further by cutting the wipes in half. (One family I know swears that an electric knife cuts through the wipes like magic!)

Show Me the Money!

Expecting more than one baby? Be sure to phone around until you find a baby store that offers a discount to parents of multiples. You're going to need nearly twice as much gear as parents with a single baby: the least the retailers can do is give you a bit of a break!

- Look for alternatives to the big brand names. If you've got the financial means and it's important to you that your child looks as cute as the babies in the Baby Gap or Osh Kosh ads, then go for it. If, however, you think it's ridiculous to spend $40 on a pair of overalls that your baby will only be able to wear for a matter of weeks, then you might want to look for good-quality generic brands instead.

- Stick to unisex colours and styles if you're planning to have more than one child. Your daughter might look cute in that frilly pink rosebud bonnet, but her future baby brother might not be able to carry off the look with quite the same style.
- Only buy clothing as you need it. That way, if someone decides to lend you her child's baby clothes, you won't have already spent a small fortune on clothing that you didn't really need.
- Be careful when you're picking up end-of-season clothes. While you might think that your chubby-cheeked six month old will be wearing a size 2 snowsuit by this time next year, it's hard to predict what size he'll actually be at that time. That $30 bargain could end up being a $30 waste of money.

From here to maternity

Your baby-to-be isn't the only one who needs a wardrobe. Expectant mothers need clothes, too. Here are some tips on putting together a budget-friendly maternity wardrobe:

- Purchase one or two items at a time rather than buying your entire wardrobe up front. Not only is it hard to predict how much your belly will blossom; it's also a nice pick-me-up to treat yourself to a new outfit during the interminably long third trimester.
- Don't spend a lot of money on maternity underwear until you're sure you're actually going to need it. A lot of women get away with wearing bikini underwear while they're pregnant.
- If you need to switch to a larger bra size while you're pregnant, buy nursing bras rather than regular bras. That way, if you plan to breastfeed your baby, you won't have to go out and buy yourself another set of bras.
- Try to shop somewhere other than the maternity stores. You can put together terrific outfits at a plus-sized retailer like Cotton Ginny Plus.
- If your husband is at least a few sizes larger than you, try raiding his side of the closet for sweaters, sweatshirts, and other oversized casual clothing.
- If you need a dress for a formal occasion, rent it rather than buying it. You'll save one-half to two-thirds of the cost.

Shopping secondhand

While you can save yourself a lot of money by shopping secondhand, you have to know what you're buying. The CBC television show *Marketplace* discovered that all kinds of dangerous baby items—items that have been off the market for years, in many cases—are readily available at garage sales.

It's not just garage sales that pose a risk to your child's safety, of course. If you find a car seat advertised on the bulletin board at your grocery store or in your local newspaper, you've also got to exercise similar caution.

Here are a few of the items that you should definitely avoid when you're shopping secondhand:

- **Humidifiers, bottle-warmers, and other small appliances:** According to the Canadian Standards Association (CSA), the problem with purchasing these items secondhand is that you have no idea how old the appliance is, whether it has been used properly or misused, and whether it meets current safety standards.

- **Cribs made before September 1986:** The problem with purchasing a secondhand crib is that you may have a hard time determining whether it complies with current safety standards. Only cribs manufactured during or after September 1986 are considered safe. Be careful buying any used crib—even if a crib is new enough to conform with safety standards, there's always the possibility that it has been damaged through misuse.

- **Playpens made before 1976:** It's unbelievable how long certain types of baby equipment remain in use, and playpens are a prime example. Even though playpen standards were revised in 1976 to ensure that mesh-sided playpens were made of mosquito-type netting with holes that are small enough to prevent a child from becoming entangled, you'll still find some prehistoric playpens kicking around at garage sales. Unless you're certain that a playpen is reasonably new and that it is in good working order (e.g., it won't collapse while your child is in it), just say no to the bargain.

- **Baby gates made before 1990:** Accordian-style baby gates with diamond-shaped openings and large Vs at the top have been off the market for nearly a decade, but you'll still find them at garage sales. Avoid them at all costs.

- **Car seats:** It's generally a bad idea to purchase a secondhand car seat. The problem is that you can never be 100 percent sure that the car seat hasn't been involved in a car accident. (Even a minor fender-bender can make a car seat unsafe.) Even if you're certain that the car seat hasn't been involved in an accident, you still need to think twice about the purchase: pass on the chance to purchase a car seat that is more than 10 years old or that is missing its installation instructions.

Show Me the Money!

Looking for a good source of secondhand children's clothing? Contact your local Parents of Twins Club and find out if they have an annual garage sale.

You can reduce the risks of shopping secondhand by dealing with a reputable secondhand children's store. In most cases, the owners of these stores make a point of rejecting items that are unsafe. That's not to say that you won't find any unsafe items, but you certainly put the odds in your favour. Regardless of where you shop, you should be prepared to ask the following questions when you're shopping secondhand:

- Who manufactured this product and when was it made?
- What is the model number?
- Where is the instruction manual?
- How many families have used it?
- Has it ever been repaired?
- Are any of the parts missing? If so, are they essential to the functioning of the product?
- Does the product conform to current safety standards?

If you would like to learn more about the ins and outs of purchasing secondhand baby equipment, contact the Infant and Toddler Safety Association (ITSA), 385 Fairway Road South, Suite 4A- 230, Kitchener, Ontario N2C 2N9; 1-519-570-0181.

Your baby's room

Every parent has visions of the perfect baby's room, but is it really necessary to spend $2,000 decorating and equipping a nursery for a tiny newborn infant who won't even care? If you'd like to create a beautiful nursery for your baby without depleting your bank account, keep the following tips in mind:

- Dress up the walls with a wallpaper border. If you're not exactly the Martha Stewart type but you can't afford to wallpaper the room, combine painted walls with a wallpaper border at either hip or ceiling height. (It'll wear better at ceiling height, but your baby will be able to enjoy the border more if you hang it roughly two-thirds of the way down the wall.)

Show Me the Money!

Here's a fun and inexpensive way to decorate your baby's room. Invite friends and relatives to come over and dip their hands into a bucket of paint and then make handprints on the wall. They can then sign their names underneath.

- If you decide to spring for wallpaper, invest in the good stuff—a high-quality scrubbable vinyl—and choose a pattern that won't look too baby-ish in a few years' time. Pastel ducks may look cute now, but just try to convince your five-year-old boy that ducks are where it's at when he has his heart set on race cars or Power Rangers!

- The flooring you choose needs to be similarly durable. Stain-resistant carpet and hardwood floors are worth every penny when you consider the types of abuse the floor is likely to encounter during your baby's first few years. Note: If you've already got wall-to-wall carpet in the nursery and you're concerned that it might not weather your child's babyhood particularly well, an inexpensive area rug might be a good investment.

- Pass on the designer bedding. Consider what my co-author and I had to say about this particular budget item in our book *The Unofficial Guide to Having a Baby:* "Babies don't care if they're sleeping on Winnie the Pooh sheets or if they have a Mickey Mouse wallpaper border. You can save a bundle by purchasing solid-colour sheets rather than their designer equivalents and coming up with creative and inexpensive ways to decorate your baby's room."

The rest of the story

Up until now, we've been focussing on the baby portion of your budget. As hefty as these expenses can be, they're insignificant compared to some of the other big-ticket items in your budget: housing, transportation costs, food, and so on. If you're serious about reducing your spending, you'll also have to consider ways to cut costs in these and other areas, too.

How much you decide to cut your costs is something that you and your family will have to decide for yourselves. Some families choose to make far-reaching changes to their lifestyle, getting rid of the second car, looking for alternatives to high-priced prepared foods, and so on. Others prefer to make more modest cuts that don't have quite the same impact on their lifestyle. After all, dining out once a month rather than weekly can hardly be categorized as a major lifestyle change!

Show Me the Money!

Find out if there's a toy-lending library in your community. Check with your local family resource centre or the children's department of your local library. For as little as $20 per year, your baby could have access to an ever-changing parade of toys.

If you're ready to make some changes so that you'll have more money left in your bank account at the end of the month, you'll find plenty of inspiration elsewhere in this book—in Chapters 3, 5, and 6, among others. Rather than trying to make all of these changes—something that would no doubt drive your family crazy—simply pick and choose the ones that are going to deliver the maximum gain for the least pain.

Nine

DEATH AND TAXES

Death and taxes. This sure sounds like a fun chapter, doesn't it? Bet you can't wait to start reading it! While you might prefer to skip this chapter entirely rather than face up to the two ugliest truths out there—your mortality and your tax bracket—it's important that you pour yourself a stiff cup of coffee and force yourself to read on.

Let's tackle the death part first.

Once you have dependents, you are responsible for ensuring that they will be taken care of in the event that something happens to you or your partner. That means writing a will, purchasing adequate amounts of life and disability insurance, setting up powers of attorney, and ensuring that your estate won't be subject to any more income tax or probate fees than absolutely necessary. This whole process of putting your affairs in order is known as estate planning.

A recent study by Royal Trust indicated that nearly half of Canadian adults don't have a will.

Where there's a will...

Sitting down to write a will certainly isn't the most pleasant task in the world, but it's certainly a necessary one. If you don't have a will, you give up the right to choose your estate's beneficiaries, make gifts to close friends, name the executor of your estate, and designate a guardian for your children. (You can find a concise summary of the laws in each province in Table 9.1.) To make matters worse, your estate would also end up taking a bigger financial hit than it might otherwise have taken: more income tax and higher probate fees.

While you'll find all kinds of do-it-yourself will kits in bookstores and stationery stores, it's generally a good idea to get legal advice when you're putting together your will—something that will cost you at most a couple of hundred dollars. There's simply too much on the line to cut corners in this important area.

Table 9.1: What happens if you die without a will?

Province	If you have a spouse and one child	If you have a spouse and more than one child	If you have children but no spouse
Newfoundland	Your estate is split equally between your spouse and your child.	One-third of your estate goes to your spouse and two-thirds to your children.	Your entire estate goes to your children.
Nova Scotia	The first $50,000 of your estate (or the house and its contents) goes to your spouse; the remainder of the estate is split equally between your spouse and your child.	The first $50,000 of your estate (or the house and its contents) goes to your spouse; the remainder is split between your spouse and your children, with one-third going to your spouse and two-thirds going to your children.	Your entire estate goes to your children.
Prince Edward Island	Your estate is split equally between your spouse and your child.	One-third of your estate goes to your spouse and two-thirds to your children.	Your entire estate goes to your children.
New Brunswick	Marital property goes to your spouse; the rest of your estate is split equally between your spouse and your child.	Marital property goes to your spouse; the rest of your estate is split equally between your spouse and your children.	Your entire estate goes to your children.

continued...

Province	If you have a spouse and one child	If you have a spouse and more than one child	If you have children but no spouse
Quebec	One-third of your estate goes to your spouse and two-thirds to your child (subject to the provisions of Bill 146, Economic Equality Between Spouses).	One-third of your estate goes to your spouse and two-thirds to your children (subject to provisions of Bill 146, Economic Equality Between Spouses).	Your entire estate goes to your children.
Ontario	The first $200,000 goes to your spouse and two-thirds to your child (subject to a possible euqalization claim under the Family Law Act); the rest of your estate is split equally between your spouse and your child.	The first $200,00 goes to your spouse (subject to a possible equal-ization claim under the Family Law Act); the rest of your estate is split between your spouse and your children, with your spouse receiving 1/3 and your children receiving 2/3.	Your entire estate goes to your children.
Manitoba	If your surviving child is also the child of the surviving spouse, all of your estate goes to your spouse. If your surviving child is not the child of the sur-viving spouse, the greater of $50,000 or half of the estate goes to the spouse (along with a life interest in the home plus a possible equal-ization payment under the Marital Property Act). The rest of your estate is then split equally between your spouse and your child.	If all of the surviving children are also children of the surviving spouse, all of your estate goes to your spouse. If any of the children are not also the children of the surviving spouse, the greater of $50,000 or half of the estate goes to the spouse (along with a life interest in the home plus a possible equalization payment under the Marital Property Act). The rest of your estate is then split equally between your spouse and your children.	Your entire estate goes to your children.

continued...

Province	If you have a spouse and one child	If you have a spouse and more than one child	If you have children but no spouse
Saskatchewan	The first $100,000 of your estate goes to your spouse; the remainder of the estate is split equally between your spouse and your child.	The first $100,00 of your estate goes to your spouse; the remainder of the estate is split between your spouse and your children, with one-third going to your spouse and two-thirds going to your children.	Your entire estate goes to your children.
Alberta	The first $40,000 of your estate goes to your spouse; the remainder of the estate is split equally between your spouse and your child.	The first $40,000 of your estate goes to your spouse; the remainder of the estate is split equally between your children, with one-third going to your spouse and two-thirds going to your children.	Your entire estate goes to your children.
British Columbia	The first $65,000 of your estate goes to your spouse; the remainder of the estate is split equally between your spouse and your child.	The first $65,000 of your estate goes to your spouse; the remainder of the estate is split between your spouse and your children, with one-third going to your spouse and two-thirds going to your children.	Your entire estate goes to your children.

Note: If one or more of your children are deceased but have children of their own, they are entitled to your child's share of your estate.

Source: *Maclean's Guide to Personal Finance 1999*.

What types of information should my will contain?

A typical will contains the following types of information:

- An introductory paragraph that indicates whose will it is (e.g., your name and your city, county, and province of residence).
- A statement indicating that you revoke all previous wills.

- A statement indicating who your executor and alternate executors should be.
- A statement giving the executors the right to use their discretion in either selling or not selling any of your noncash assets.
- A statement giving your executors permission to pay your debts and death-related expenses out of the proceeds of your estate.
- A statement giving your executors permission to transfer the balance of your estate to your partner, if he or she survives you for a period of 30 days, or to a trust that shall be established on behalf of your children.
- A statement in which you appoint a guardian to care for your children in the event that you and your partner die.
- The signatures of two witnesses (neither of whom should be beneficiaries of the will).

See the sample will for an example of how a will is typically structured and written.

THIS IS THE LAST WILL AND TESTAMENT of me, JANE DOE, of the City of Mississauga, in the County of Peel, and Province of Ontario.

1. I HEREBY REVOKE all Wills and testamentary dispositions of every nature or kind whatsoever by me heretofore made.

2. I NOMINATE, CONSTITUTE, AND APPOINT my husband, JOHN DOE, to be the sole executor and trustee of this my Will, but if my said husband should predecease me or die without having proved this my Will or should he at any time be unable or unwilling to act or continue to so act as my executor and trustee then on the happening of any such event I NOMINATE, CONSTITUTE, AND APPOINT my father, ROBERT BLACK, and my spouse's mother, MARY WHITE, jointly (or the survivor of them) to be the executors and trustees of this my Will in the place and stead of my said husband, and I hereinafter refer to my executor and trustee or executors and trustees for the time being as my "trustees."

3. I GIVE, DEVISE, AND BEQUEATH all my property of every nature and kind and wheresoever situated, including any property over which I have a general power of appointment to my trustees, upon the following trusts, namely:

a. To use their discretion in the realization of my estate, with power to my trustees to sell, call in and convert into money any part of my estate not consisting of money at such time or times, in such manner and upon such terms, and either for cash or credit or for part cash and part credit as my said trustees may in their uncontrolled discretion decide upon, or to postpone such conversion of my estate or any part or parts thereof for such length of time as they may think best, and I hereby declare that my said trustees may retain any portion of my estate in the form in which it may be at my death as an investment of my estate (notwithstanding that it may not be in the form of an investment in which trustees are authorized to invest trust funds, whether or not there is a liability attached to any such portion of my estate) for such length of time as my said trustees may in their discretion deem advisable and my trustees shall not be held responsible for any loss that may happen to my estate by reason of their so doing.

b. To pay out of and charge to the capital of my general estate, my just debts, funeral and testamentary expenses, and all estate, inheritance and succession duties or taxes whether imposed by or pursuant to the law of this or any other jurisdiction whatsoever that may be payable in connection with any property passing (or deemed so to pass by any governing law) on my death or in connection with any insurance on my life or any gift or benefit given or conferred by me either during my lifetime or by survivorship or by this my Will or any Codicil thereto and whether such duties or taxes be payable in respect of estates or interests which fall into possession at my death or at any subsequent time; and I hereby authorize my trustees to commute or prepare any such taxes or duties.

c. To pay or transfer the residual of my estate to my said spouse, JOHN DOE, if he survives me for a period of thirty (30) days, for his own use absolutely.

d. If my said spouse should predecease me, or should survive me but die within a period of thirty days after my decease, I direct my trustees to hold the residue of my estate in trust for my issue alive at the death of the survivor of me and my said spouse in equal shares per stirpes, provided that such share of each child of mine who shall be living at the death of the survivor of me and my said spouse shall be held and kept invested by my trustees and the income and capital or so much thereof as my trustees in their uncontrolled discretion consider advisable shall be paid to or applied for the maintenance, benefit, and education of such child until he or she attains the age of twenty-one years when such share shall be paid or transferred to him or her. If any child of mine should predecease the survivor of me and my said spouse or should die before becoming entitled to receive the whole of his or her share in my estate leaving issue surviving such deceased child of mine would have taken in living. If any such deceased child should leave no child him or her surviving my surviving children shall take in equal shares per stirpes that share such deceased child of mine would have taken if living.

e. In case no child or other issue of mine shall acquire an absolutely vested interest by virtue of the trusts herein declared I direct my trustees to divide the residue of my estate into two (2) equal shares, one of such equal shares to be paid or transferred to my parents, or the survivor of them, and the other equal share to be paid or transferred to my spouse's parents, or the survivor of them.

4. IF ANY PERSON should become entitled to any share in my estate before attaining the age of twenty-one (21) years, the share of such person shall be held and kept invested by my trustees and the income and capital or so much thereof as my trustees in their absolute discretion consider necessary or advisable shall be used for the benefit of such person until he or she attains the age of twenty-one (21) years.

5. I AUTHORIZE my trustees to make any payments for any persons under the age of eighteen (18) years to a parent or guardian of such person whose receipt shall be a sufficient discharge to my said trustees.

6. IT IS MY EXPRESS intention that any income from a bequest given in connection with the provisions of my Will shall be excluded from my beneficiaries' net family property as defined in The Family Law Act, Ontario, 1985.

7. IN THE CASE of the death of my said spouse, JOHN DOE, and myself during the infancy of any child of mine, I APPOINT my parents, ROBERT WILLIAM BLACK AND RACHEL JANET BLACK, to be the custodians and guardians of the persons and estates of such child during his or her respective minority.

IN TESTIMONY WHEREOF, I have to this my Last Will and Testament written upon this and three (3) preceding pages of paper subscribed my name this 15 day of January, A.D., 1999.

SIGNED, PUBLISHED, AND DECLARED by the said JANE DOE as and for her last will and testament in the presence of us both present at the same time who at her request and in her presence and in the presence of each other have hereunto subscribed our names as witnesses.

_____

Signature

_____   _____

Name   Name

_____   _____

Address   Address

_____   _____

Occupation   Occupation

What factors do I need to consider in choosing an executor for my will?

You should put a lot of thought into choosing an executor. Don't just pick your brother because you think you should: look for someone who is trustworthy, astute at handling money, and a good administrator. The responsibilities that will need to be carried out by the executor of your will include

- burying you or disposing of your remains
- collecting any money that is owed to your estate
- paying all the debts owed by the estate (including income and estate taxes)
- taking inventory of your assets and
- distributing the assets to the beneficiaries of your will

It's a good idea to pick someone who is your age or younger than you rather than choosing one of your parents. Odds are, they'll die first.

Facts and Figures

Your executor is entitled to charge a fee of up to five percent for managing your estate and for overseeing your trust.

What factors do I need to consider in choosing a guardian for my children?

If there's one aspect of the whole estate planning process that you're going to find particularly upsetting, this is it. It's painful enough even to consider the possibility that you might not be able to watch your child grow up. It's a thousand times worse to have to choose someone else to step into your shoes. And even if you know in your heart that your sister would be the perfect guardian for your children, she may not be willing or able to take on this role. After all, you're not just asking her to watch your kids for the weekend. You're asking her to watch over them for the rest of their lives!

While it's never easy to choose a guardian, it's an essential part of the estate planning process. If you were to die without designating a guardian for your children, the province would end up doing it on your behalf—a very scary thought indeed. Here are a few points to keep in mind as you consider who would—and wouldn't—be a suitable guardian for your children:

- **Childrearing philosophies:** It's a good idea to choose a guardian who shares your parenting philosophies. That way, you'll know that, should anything happen to you and your partner, your children will be brought up in a similar fashion to the way you intended to raise them.

- **Age:** While you might be tempted to choose your parents or your partner's parents as guardians, it's best if you can find someone younger to take on this role. There's a world of difference between being a grandparent and a parent. Unless your parents or your in-laws have expressed their willingness to become your children's guardian and they are healthy and energetic enough to take on childrearing responsibilities again, you might want to consider appointing someone else instead.
- **Your child's relationship with this person:** If your child absolutely adores your sister-in-law, then she may be a shoo-in for the position of guardian. If, on the other hand, your child drives her crazy and she has no patience with him, you might want to rethink your decision to appoint her as his guardian.
- **Willingness to accept the job:** Not everyone is willing to act as the guardian for someone else's children. Just as you wouldn't dream of nominating your best friend for political office without talking with her about it first, you shouldn't name anyone your child's guardian without first having a heart-to-heart talk about it. Don't be surprised if the would-be guardian says no: after all, you're not just asking her to stay with your kids for a week. You're asking her to become your child's parent for life.

Note: You should always name an alternate guardian in your will, just in case your first choice is unable or unwilling to step in. And if you happen to name a married couple as your child's guardian, be sure to indicate which member of the couple would continue to be your child's guardian in the event that they were to separate or divorce.

Show Me the Money!

Some financial planners recommend that you include some wording in your will that would provide your children's trustee with greater investment options than are normally allowed under the terms of provincial trustee acts. It's a point worth raising with both your lawyer and your financial advisor when you're having your will drawn up.

How often should I update my will?

You should review your will at least once every five years—sooner if your circumstances change. Circumstances in which you would want to write a new will include

- if you were to divorce or remarry
- if you were to become a parent for the first time
- if you changed your name or anyone mentioned in the will changed their name
- if your executor were to die or become incapable of performing the duties of executor
- if one of your beneficiaries were to die
- if you were to sell any of the property that you have bequeathed under the terms of your will

What is a power of attorney and where does it fit into the estate planning picture?

A power of attorney is a document that gives someone authority to act on your behalf in the event that you become incapacitated and are no longer capable of making decisions on your own. There are actually two types of powers of attorney: a power of attorney to deal with financial matters and a power of attorney to make healthcare decisions (e.g., to request that you be taken off life-support machines, if that is your choice).

Every adult should have a power of attorney set up years before he or she actually needs it. In most cases, your lawyer will recommend that you set it up at the same time that you're writing your will. If you are in a stable relationship, you will probably decide to assign your power of attorney to your partner. If you're not, you might choose to assign it to a trusted relative (e.g., your brother or your sister) instead.

What is a terminal tax return?

A terminal tax return is the final tax return you ever have to file—the one that your executor files on your behalf within six months of April 30 of the year following your death (June 15 if you or your spouse are self-employed). It's your final chance to settle up with the folks at Revenue Canada, who are gleefully waiting with their hands open. You may also be able to file a special additional tax return for dividends declared but unpaid; salaries, commissions and vacation pay owing but unpaid; and so on. Consult a tax accountant for advice on this particular area of tax law.

If you think you pay too much tax right now, wait till you find out what happens when Revenue Canada gets its hands on your assets after you die.

the Bottom line

Upon your death, Revenue Canada treats your capital assets as if they have been sold at their current fair market value, even if your heirs decide to hold on to them instead, as they might decide to do with a family cottage. As a result, your estate could end up taking a major tax hit and your heirs could be forced to sell off assets in order to come up with the necessary cash to pay Revenue Canada.

Here's a list of some of the major types of income that will be included in your final tax return:

- **Income received during the year:** The executor who files your final tax return will have to include all income you received from employment, investment, or other sources during your final tax year.

- **RRSPs:** The full value of your RRSPs is included as income unless your beneficiary happens to be your spouse, in which case the RRSP qualifies for a spousal rollover (which simply means that your spouse—or a minor or infirm child, if you don't have a spouse—is able to transfer your RRSP funds to his or her RRSP account.) Note: In Quebec, in order for the designation to be valid, you must name your spouse as your RRSP beneficiary in your will.

- **RRIFs:** The fair market value of your registered retirement income funds (RRIFs) is treated as income in the year of your death unless you have a surviving spouse or dependent child.

- **Capital property:** Your capital property is treated as if it has been sold off at fair market value. Consequently, if your property has increased in value, you may end up paying taxes on this "income" (the increased value of the property).

- **Registered Pension Plans:** In some cases, the death benefit you receive under a registered pension plan (RRP) may be taxable, for example if you have no spouse or designated beneficiary.

Money Talk

"Anything you leave to your spouse won't be taxed, but some of those taxes, particularly taxes on capital gains, aren't forgotten; they're simply deferred. They'll have to be paid eventually, either when your spouse sells the assets or dies."
Source: Elaine Wyatt, *The Money Companion.*

It's not all bad news, of course. Believe it or not, Revenue Canada does give you the odd break:

- Your estate can take advantage of the principal residence exemption in order to avoid paying taxes on your house.
- You're allowed to deduct any net capital losses from your overall income (as opposed to just deducting it from any taxable capital gains, as is normally the case).
- Your spouse can make a contribution on your behalf to a spousal RRSP within 60 days of the end of the calendar year in which your death occurred.

Show Me the Money!

Be sure to keep some cash in your own name. That way, if the bank freezes the joint chequing account upon the death of your partner, you'll still have money to live on until your partner's estate is settled.

What can I do to reduce the probate fees that have to be paid on my estate?

You already know what income tax is. You've had the pleasure of paying it since the day you received your first paycheque. You might be less clear about what probate fees are. Probate is the legal process of administering and implementing the directions in a will, and probate fees are the government's charges on the property covered by the will.

There's no way to beat probate fees altogether, but there are a few things you can do to lessen the blow. For starters, you should make sure that bank accounts, brokerage accounts, RRSPs, RRIFs, and any properties you own are jointly held by you and one of your beneficiaries. (Be careful! To be legitimate in the eyes of the government, the beneficiary must be a legal owner of the asset or property in question. You may or may not be willing to put some of you biggest assets in the name of your 18-year-old son!) These assets won't have to go through probate; they'll simply pass directly from you to your beneficiary. That can save you a considerable amount of money, since probate fees can range as high as 1.5 percent in some provinces.

You should also give some thought to investing a portion of your estate in segregated funds (investment funds that are run by insurance companies). These funds bypass all estate and legal fees. What's more, they provide you with added protection in the event of a bankruptcy.

the Bottom line

If you and your partner own a home, make sure that it's set up "as joint tenants with right of survivorship." This means that if one of you were to die tomorrow, the other would own the house outright. If you held the property as "tenants in common," it's the will of the deceased person that determines who gets his or her share of the house and, even worse, the house has to go through the costly probate process.

Life Insurance 101

Now that we've talked about the ins and outs of wills and other aspects of estate planning, let's zero in on a topic that's equally important, but that most Canadians find both boring and baffling: life insurance.

How much life insurance do I need?

The purpose of life insurance is to provide for your family after your death. Whether you're a stay-at-home parent or a working parent, your family depends on your contributions—paid and unpaid—to maintain its current standard of living.

You may be surprised by the value of your contributions. As you work through the calculations in Table 9.2, you will see just how significant a financial impact your family would face if you were to die suddenly. Table 9.3 will give you an idea of the total investment required to replace your contribution to your family's income.

Table 9.2: How much life insurance do you need?

		You	Your partner
Liabilities			
Mortgage		_____	_____
Car loans		_____	_____
Other debt		_____	_____
Total liabilities	(a)	_____	_____
Cash needs			
Final expenses (burial, taxes, probate fees, legal fees)		_____	_____

continued...

Table 9.2: How much life insurance do you need?

		You	Your partner
Your children's education		_____	_____
Childcare expenses		_____	_____
Eldercare expenses (important if you're responsible for caring for an aging parent)		_____	_____
Other cash needs (e.g., emergency fund)		_____	_____
Total cash needs	(b)	_____	_____
Amount of money required to replace lost income			
Gross annual income required by family	(c)	_____	_____
Gross annual income of partner (if applicable)	(d)	_____	_____
Annual income shortage or surplus (figure c – figure d)	(e)	_____	_____
Assumed rate of return on investment (adjust for inflation, if desired, using Table 9.3)	(f)	_____	_____
Amount of money needed to make up income shortage (figure e divided by figure f)	(g)	_____	_____
Total amount of money required without factoring in assets (figure b plus figure g)	(h)	_____	_____
Adjustment for family assets			
Cash savings (savings, T-bills, Canada Savings Bonds, etc.)		_____	_____
RRSPs (note: these can be rolled over to your partner)		_____	_____
Stocks, bonds, and mutual funds		_____	_____
Your house (principal residence only)		_____	_____
Life insurance (total of all policies: group, personal, mortgage, credit)		_____	_____
Business assets (if applicable)		_____	_____
CPP/QPP death benefit and any pension plan death benefits		_____	_____
Total amount available	(i)	_____	_____
Total amount required	(j)	_____	_____

Source: Adapted from a life insurance worksheet developed by the Manufacturers Life Insurance Company.

Table 9.3: Money required to provide various levels of monthly income at various interest rates

Annual income	Monthly income	Total investment required			
		Interest rate			
		4%	6%	8%	10%
$12,000	$1,000	$300,000	$200,000	$150,000	$120,000
15,000	1,250	375,000	250,000	187,500	150,000
18,000	1,500	450,000	300,000	225,000	180,000
21,000	1,750	525,000	350,000	262,500	210,000
24,000	2,000	600,000	400,000	300,000	240,000
27,000	2,250	675,000	450,000	337,500	270,000
30,000	2,500	750,000	500,000	375,000	300,000
33,000	2,750	825,000	550,000	412,500	330,000
36,000	3,000	900,000	600,000	450,000	360,000
39,000	3,250	975,000	650,000	487,500	390,000
42,000	3,500	1,050,000	700,000	525,000	420,000
45,000	3,750	1,125,000	750,000	562,500	450,000
48,000	4,000	1,200,000	800,000	600,000	480,000
51,000	4,250	1,275,000	850,000	637,500	510,000
54,000	4,500	1,350,000	900,000	675,000	540,000
57,000	4,750	1,425,000	950,000	712,500	570,000
60,000	5,000	1,500,000	1,000,000	750,000	600,000

Note: If you wish to adjust for inflation, simply subtract the projected rate of inflation from the projected rate of return and look up the difference on this table.

Source: Manufacturers Life Insurance Company.

the Bottom line

Resist the temptation to buy into a group life insurance plan without taking the time to read all the fine print. If you're in good health, you could end up subsidizing the insurance costs of other less healthy members of the group. What's more, if the plan ended up being a money-losing venture for the insurer, they could choose to cancel it, which could leave you scrambling to find a new insurer and/or left with no insurance at all!

Whom should I choose as a beneficiary?

If you are married or living common law, you will probably name your partner as the beneficiary of your life insurance policy and list your children as alternate beneficiaries. It's important to change the beneficiaries on your policy if your life circumstances change (e.g., if you and your partner separate or if your partner dies). Usually this is simply a matter of filling out an insurance company form, but if you've purchased a policy with an irrevocably designated beneficiary, you would have to obtain that person's consent to change beneficiaries—something that could prove extremely difficult if you were in the middle of a particularly difficult divorce proceeding.

If you have young children, you might want to consider bypassing your partner altogether by setting up a trust to receive and manage any proceeds from your insurance policy on their behalf until they are older. A financial planner can help you to decide if it would be in your best interests to do so.

Whatever you do, don't die without naming a beneficiary on your insurance policy. If this were to happen, there would be a delay in releasing the funds to your heirs and, what's more, the proceeds of the policy would be considered part of your estate, which would make them subject to probate fees and legal fees.

Facts and Figures

The Canadian Life and Health Insurance Association Inc. operates a free consumer helpline to answer your questions about insurance. It operates from 9:00 a.m. to 5:00 p.m. eastern time from Monday to Friday. You can reach the hotline by calling 1-800-268-8099.

What type of insurance should I buy?

When you're shopping for life insurance, you have two basic choices: term policies and cash value policies.

Term insurance is basic, no-frills insurance designed to offer the most bang for the least buck. Your premium is determined by such factors as the amount of coverage you want (e.g., $50,000 or $500,000 worth of coverage, or some other amount entirely), your age, and your health at the time when you purchase the insurance.

Here are some questions to ask your insurance agent when you're evaluating a particular term insurance policy:

- **How often does the premium change?** Not surprisingly, your premiums increase as you age. Some policy premiums increase annually; others only increase every so many years (e.g., every ten years). The advantage of having a premium that's locked in for ten years is that you'll know exactly what you're paying over that period. The disadvantage is that you may end up paying more than you might otherwise have paid during the first few years of the term.

- **Is the policy guaranteed to be renewable?** Guaranteed renewability ensures that your life insurance policy can't be cancelled by the insurer if your health takes a turn for the worst. Don't even think about buying an insurance policy without this guarantee or you could find yourself without insurance at the very time when you need it most.

- **What will the renewal rate be?** The best term life insurance policies map out what you will pay each time you renew your insurance policy. If you don't have this type of guarantee written into your policy, your insurance costs could skyrocket at renewal time.

- **Is the policy guaranteed to be convertible?** Another important feature to shop for is guaranteed conversion. This means that you can make the jump from term insurance (which gets more expensive over time) to cash value insurance (where your premiums are fixed over time) without having to go for the usual medical examination.

  Here's some more term insurance lingo that you need to know about:

- *Annual renewable term insurance* means that the premium you pay will increase each year when you renew your policy. This is generally the least expensive type of term insurance.

- *Level coverage* means that your premiums are guaranteed to remain level for a period of time—five, ten, or twenty years, for example—increasing only when the specified term expires.

- *Credit (or mortgage) insurance* refers to life insurance that you have taken out to cover a particular loan or mortgage. The amount of coverage you are receiving decreases as the loan or mortgage balance goes down, but your payments remain the same or increase. This is the most expensive type of term insurance.

Facts and Figures

Are you separated or divorced? Make sure you have enough life insurance to cover any support payments you are required by law to make. More often than not, your estate will be obligated to continue making those payments after your death.

Cash value life insurance—sometimes referred to as permanent or whole-life insurance—is four to ten times as expensive as term insurance. This is because you deliberately overpay into the plan so that you can build up a surplus of savings. Most people either love or hate cash value insurance. Those who aren't particularly motivated savers like it because it forces them to save money on a regular basis. More savvy investors tend to give cash value life insurance the thumbs down, arguing that it's overpriced and that they can earn a better return on their money by investing their funds on their own.

There are three basic terms you need to know when you're shopping for life insurance: whole life coverage, universal coverage, and variable life coverage.

With whole life coverage you will pay the same premium for as long as you hold the policy, and you know in advance what your death benefit will be. Part of each payment you make is invested on your behalf. As your savings increase, you are able to borrow against the cash value of the policy. You can either continue paying your premiums well into your old age or you can have the premiums taken out of the accumulated cash value of the policy after a certain number of years—a feature that is referred to in the industry as "vanishing premiums."

If you choose universal coverage, you are able to determine how much of your premium will be used to cover your insurance costs and how much will be set aside for savings. The key advantage of this type of plan is its flexibility: you can change the premium payment or the amount of the death benefit at any time. The key disadvantage is that this type of life insurance can be costly. Note: If the savings component of the plan grows, you may be able to pay the policy premiums using the money your investments have earned within the policy.

If you choose variable life coverage, your premiums are fixed, but the death benefit that you can receive rises and falls based on the performance of the insurance company's investments. However, your death benefit will not drop below the original amount of insurance coverage you purchased, as specified in your policy. These types of policies aren't sold as often as they once were.

As you can see, cash value insurance is a complex topic. You'll definitely want to zero in on the pros and cons of any particular policy you're considering. As Steve Maple and Edward Olkovich point out in *The Complete Idiot's Guide to Wills and Estates for Canadians*, "What the large print giveth, the small print often taketh away."

Money Talk

"If you are married, it's better to purchase a joint first-to-die insurance policy. This covers you and your spouse, but pays off in the death of the first person. This strategy can save you five to ten percent over the cost of purchasing two separate policies—$75 to $125 per year for a typical policyholder."

Source: Robert K. Heady, Christy Heady, and Bruce McDougall, *The Complete Idiot's Guide to Managing Your Money in Canada.*

Disability insurance

Disability insurance is the Rodney Dangerfield of the insurance world: it doesn't get any respect. A surprising number of people go to great lengths to insure themselves against the ultimate disaster—death—but fail to protect themselves and their families against a more likely catastrophe—temporary or permanent disability.

Here are a few hair-raising statistics on the disability insurance front:

- One-third of all disabilities are suffered by people under the age of 45. What's more, the majority of disabilities are caused by medical problems or accidents that can't be predicted in advance.
- Being disabled for a single year can wipe out a decade's worth of savings.
- Fewer than half of Canadian workers are covered by disability insurance.
- Approximately 43 percent of all loan and property foreclosures are the result of a disability.

While it's tempting to think that Big Brother—the federal government—will take care of you and your family if you suffer a permanent disability, the amount of support that you could expect to receive through either the Canada Pension Plan or Quebec Pension Plan or through worker's compensation is minimal to say the least. (Don't forget: not all workers are covered through worker's compensation, and there's always the chance that you could be injured off the job, in which case you wouldn't be covered by worker's compensation at all. What's more, worker's compensation covers injury only—not sickness.)

When you're shopping around for disability insurance, you'll need to know how long you will require the coverage (e.g., until you're 65 and you can access your retirement savings, for example) and how much income you need to replace each year. Then you'll need to get out your magnifying glass and read the fine print on the policy. Here's what to look for:

- **A reasonable definition of disability.** Some policies are so rigid about the definition of disability that it's almost impossible to make a claim. Look for a policy with an "own-occupation" or "regular-occupation" disability clause. Other types of policies require you to work at any position for which you are reasonably trained rather than staying off work until you're well enough to return to your usual occupation. Obviously you pay more for own-occupation coverage, but if you're in a reasonably well-paid profession and you'd have to take a big pay cut to switch to a career in any sort of related work, you'd probably be wise to spring for this kind of coverage.

- **Noncancellable and guaranteed renewable.** As the terms imply, you want a policy that cannot be cancelled by the insurer either before or at the time of renewal because you are in poor health. Otherwise, you could find yourself losing your coverage at the very time when you need it most.

- **Waiting period.** To keep your disability premiums as low as possible, look for a policy with a long waiting period (the amount of time you have to wait until benefits kick in). Obviously, you'll want to take into account how much savings you have on hand since you'll be using your nest egg to stay afloat during this time period. While the waiting period on most policies is 30 days, some go as high as one to two years. A three- to six-month waiting period is ideal if you can afford it.

- **Residual benefits.** Look for a policy that will provide you with partial benefits if you are able to work part-time but not full-time.

- **Cost-of-living adjustments.** Over time, inflation can erode the amount of your disability insurance payments. That's why it's important to choose a policy that will be adjusted by either a set percentage each year or by the amount of inflation.

Show Me the Money!

Don't assume that your job is finished once you settle on an insurance or disability policy. The experts recommend that you review your insurance needs at least every couple of years to ensure that your coverage still matches your current needs.

As you can see, there's a lot involved in protecting your family and your estate from disaster. You need to write a will, assign power of attorney to your partner or another trusted person, do what you can to minimize the tax consequences and probate costs associated with your death, and shop around for the right type and amount of life and disability insurance. It can be a time-consuming and difficult process, but you owe it to your family to do it right.

Ten

LIFE AFTER CHILDREN

As hard as it may be to believe right now, the day will come when your children grow up and leave home. Instead of tripping over dinky cars and wiping up juice spills, you could find yourself living a positively Martha Stewartesque lifestyle. (That last bit may be pure fantasy. If you've been a slob all your life, it's unlikely that you're going to suddenly morph into a domestic diva.)

What I'm trying to say is that the years when you have your children living at home with you are a very short time in your life—generally 20 years or less. (Sure, some adult children return to the nest for short periods of time if they find themselves out of work or in the midst of a messy divorce, but at that point they're more like tenants than children.) That's why it's important to start thinking now about what your life will be like when your children have left the nest and to plan your future accordingly.

Money Talk

"When we were first married and had no children, saving for retirement was a high priority. However, when the children arrived, our priorities changed. We now have to save for braces, post-secondary education and so on. We still save for retirement, but not as much as we did before. We will let compound interest work for us for now."
– Leigh, 31, mother of two.

The not-so-golden years

It's one thing to dream of travelling and enjoying life during your retirement years. It's another to start the financial planning process soon enough make those dreams a reality. If you're serious about wanting to retire early or to maintain your current lifestyle after you retire, you're going to have to get serious about saving hefty chunks of your income now. (See Table 10.1 for some basic guidelines.)

Table 10.1: How much you need to save each year

This table shows the percentage of your income you need to start saving today to have an annual retirement income of half the salary you earn during your last year in the workforce at the age you hope to retire.

	Percentage of income to save		
	Retire at 60	Retire at 65	Retire at 70
If you start saving at age 20	19%	14%	10%
If you start saving at age 25	22%	16%	11%
If you start saving at age 30	25%	18%	13%
If you start saving at age 35	30%	21%	15%
If you start saving at age 40	38%	25%	17%
If you start saving at age 45		31%	20%
If you start saving at age 50			25%

Note: These figures are based on the assumption that your salary will increase two percent more than inflation each year and that your savings are earning a return of at least two percent more than inflation in a pension or RRSP.

Source: Adapted from Elaine Wyatt, *The Money Companion*. Original table created by Frank Russell of Canada Ltd.

Another way to figure out how much money you'll need during your retirement years is to turn to the ever-growing number of studies on the amount of income required to maintain a pre-retirement lifestyle past age 65. Here are a few statistics from *Personal Finance for Dummies for Canadians* that are certainly worth considering:

- Studies have shown that most people need about 70 to 80 percent of their pre-retirement income if they hope to maintain their standard of living.

- You can probably get by on as little as 65 percent of your pre-retirement income if you've consistently saved 15 percent or more of your annual earnings, you are a high-income earner, your house is paid off, and you are hoping for a modest lifestyle upon retirement.

- You will probably need about 75 percent of your pre-retirement income if you have managed to save a reasonable but not spectacular amount of your annual income, you will have a small amount of - personal debt to pay off during your retirement years and/or rent to pay on a house or apartment, and you are hoping to enjoy the same standard of living during your retirement years as you are enjoying today.

Facts and Figures

A recent study indicated that two-thirds of Canadians believe that government programs will not be able to provide them with a secure retirement income.
Source: Personal Finance for Dummies for Canadians.

- You will need approximately 85 percent of your pre-retirement income if you have managed to save very little money over the years (less than 5 percent of your annual earnings), you have a significant mortgage payment or a sizeable and growing rent payment, and you want or need to maintain your current lifestyle during your retirement years.

If you'd like to do a more detailed calculation to figure out how much money you should be saving today, simply rework the budget that you prepared back in Chapter 2. Some of the major types of expenses that will increase or decrease significantly once you retire include

- groceries
- restaurant expenses
- clothing
- laundry and dry cleaning
- transportation costs
- travel
- entertainment
- hobbies
- books and magazines
- life insurance premiums
- medical insurance premiums
- disability insurance premiums
- car insurance premiums
- dental bills

Once you've worked out the budget for your retirement years, you'll need to factor in inflation. You can do this by using the college costs inflation table in Chapter 7.

Your next step is to compare your projected expenses with your projected income. Tally up the income you expect to receive from such sources as Old Age Security, the Canada Pension Plan or Quebec Pension Plan, any private pensions you belong to, any deferred profit-sharing plans you participate in, your investment income, and earnings from any part-time work you intend to do in your retirement years; and then figure out what your after-tax income will be. The shortfall is the amount that you will need to make up through your own retirement savings.

Show Me the Money!

You can start collecting CPP/QPP benefits as early as age 60 or you can choose to delay payments until age 70. If you go for the early-bird plan, your benefits will be reduced by 0.5 percent for each month you retire before age 65. If you go for the deferred-gratification plan, your benefits will be increased by the corresponding amount after age 65.

Unfortunately, what this figure won't tell you—and what I certainly can't tell you—is how you're supposed to accomplish this bit of financial wizardry while you're simultaneously saving for your children's education, paying off your mortgage, and keeping the bill collectors at bay. I don't think you can make serious inroads with all of these financial goals at the same time unless you and your partner have a combined income that is significantly higher than average. If, like me, you don't fall into that category, then it's a case of playing one priority off against the and deciding just how much you can reasonably afford to save toward your retirement during this financially challenging period in your life.

What you can expect to get from government coffers

If you're expecting to live the high life on the money that you receive from the Canada Pension Plan/Quebec Pension Plan (CPP/QPP) and Old Age Security (OAS) programs, you could be in for a rude awakening. In 1998, the maximum amount that you could receive under both programs was $1,153 per month, and if you were a high-income senior, some of that money was clawed back (taxed back by the government). You must have had earned income to qualify for the CPP/QPP (worth a maximum of $744.79 per month in 1998), but anyone over the age of 65 who has lived in Canada for at least 10 years qualifies for the OAS (worth $408.78 per month in July 1998).

RRSP magic

One of the most attractive tax breaks available to Canadians is the registered retirement savings plan (RRSP). Under the current rules, you're allowed to contribute up to 18 percent of your earned income in the previous year, up to a maximum of $13,500 per year. Your taxable income for the year is reduced by the amount of money you contribute to your RRSP and the money within your RRSP grows tax-free until it is withdrawn.

It's important to understand the ins and outs of RRSPs if you're going to take full advantage of them. Here are a few more important points:

- You are only allowed to contribute 18 percent of your earned income—income such as salary, bonuses, commissions, net business income, retirement allowances, alimony and maintenance payments, net rental income, royalties, disability pensions, and certain types of taxable employment incomes, including disability and sick benefits. You're not allowed to make contributions on income from pension benefits, investments, family allowance and child tax credit payments, unemployment insurance payments, adult training allowances, and money from an income-averaging annuity.

- If you belong to a pension plan at work, your RRSP contribution limit is reduced by the value of your and your company's contributions to your employee pension plan. This figure is known as your pension adjustment.

the Bottom line

Make sure that you understand what type of pension plan you have at work. If it's a defined-benefit plan, the pension you receive will reflect your earnings and the number of years you've worked for a particular organization. If the company pension plan runs short of funds, the employer must make up the shortfall. If it's a defined-contribution plan, it's more difficult to predict how much money you will receive from the plan when you retire. How well the plan does depends on how well the money in the plan is invested. Your company pension plan administrator should be able to provide you with information about your plan.

- Your contribution limit is based on your previous year's earnings (for example, your 2000 contribution limit is based on the income you earned during the 1999 tax year) plus any unused RRSP contributions from previous years. You can calculate this figure yourself or leave this task to the folks at Revenue Canada, who notify you of your RRSP contribution room each time you file your tax return.

- You can use your RRSP as an income-splitting tool. If both partners have earned income, the spouse with the higher income can contribute to a spousal RRSP in the name of the spouse with the lower income. This will help to reduce the amount of tax you pay during your retirement years.

Show Me the Money!

Revenue Canada recently introduced a Lifelong Learning Plan (LLP). The plan allows eligible individuals to withdraw up to $10,000 per year from their RRSPs to finance full-time training or education in a qualifying educational program for themselves or their spouses. The withdrawals aren't taxable if certain conditions are met. The maximum withdrawal is $20,000 and the withdrawals must be repaid over 10 years. The Lifelong Learning Plan may not be the best way to build your retirement nest egg, but it's a nice option if you find yourself out of a job and in desperate need of retraining.

- You can take money out of your RRSP any time you like, but the income is taxable the moment it is withdrawn. The only exceptions are if you're taking advantage of the RRSP Home Buyer's Plan or the newly introduced Lifelong Learning Plan, in which case your withdrawal is tax-free provided that you adhere to the repayment rules set out in each plan. Note: If your spouse removes funds from a spousal RRSP within three years of the date of the last contribution, the proceeds are included in your (the contributor's) income.
- Canadian tax laws allow you to include a certain percentage of foreign content in your RRSPs. In general, you can earn a higher rate of return on investments outside of Canada than within the country, so make sure that you're maximizing your foreign content.
- The best way to evaluate the performance of a particular RRSP is to look at how its competitors fared over the same time period. Just make sure you're comparing apples to apples! For example, compare balanced funds to balanced funds.
- The best way to maximize the size of your RRSPs is to start contributing early (see Table 10.2 and Table 10.3).

Table 10.2: The benefits of contributing early

	The amount of money accumulated by age 65 by someone who contributes $2,000 per year for 10 years, starting at age 25, but then stops contributing	The amount of money accumulated by age 65 by someone who contributes $2,000 per year for 30 years, starting at age 35.
RRSP value at age 30	$12,671	0
RRSP value at age 34	31,290	0
RRSP value at age 40	45,975	$12,671
RRSP value at age 45	67,533	31,290
RRSP value at age 50	99,258	58,648
RRSP value at age 55	145,843	98,845
RRSP value at age 60	214,292	157,908
RRSP value at age 65	314,886	244,691

Note: The interest rate used in the above calculations is eight percent.

Source: Adapted from *RRSP: The Facts,* Manulife Financial.

Table 10.3: Annual savings needed to produce a $100,000 RRSP

The calculations in the table below assume an average annual return of 8 percent per year and a marginal tax rate of 40 percent.

Number of years left to save	Savings within an RRSP (growth is not taxed until the funds are withdrawn)	Savings outside of an RRSP (growth is taxed immediately)
5	$15,783	$17,338
10	6,392	7,657
15	3,410	4,489
20	2,023	2,947
25	1,268	2,055
30	817	1,486

Source: *The Globe and Mail.*

There are entire books devoted to the subject of RRSPs, so I've only touched on the key points in this chapter. If you're serious about maximizing your RRSP savings—and, frankly, you should be!—you should either invest in a couple more books on this topic or ask your financial planner to help you to map out the best possible strategy for achieving your retirement goals. Good luck!

Eleven

THE HOTTEST TAX BREAKS FOR
FAMILIES WITH YOUNG CHILDREN

If you're tempted to skip this chapter because you find it boring to read about the ins and outs of the Canadian income tax system, let me give you a very good reason to force yourself to struggle on: every time you fail to take advantage of a tax break, you're voluntarily handing over your hard-earned cash to every Canadian's least favourite government department: Revenue Canada.

Rather than zeroing in on the same tax breaks that every other financial planning book will tell you about, I'm going to focus on the tax breaks that are most helpful to people like you and me: parents with young children.

Facts and Figures

In 1997–98, Revenue Canada processed 5.5 million tax returns and collected $245 billion from Canadians. They also dealt with 27.2 million enquiries. (Perhaps it's time to rewrite that tax guide!)

13 tax breaks that you need to know about

There may not be a lot of tax breaks available to Canadian families, but some of them can save you a bundle. Here are the 13 best tax breaks available to Canadian parents:

RRSPs

Registered retirement savings plans are, without a doubt, the single best tax breaks available to Canadians. Contributing to an RRSP allows you to reduce your taxable income (and consequently the amount of tax you pay). The funds inside an RRSP are allowed to grow tax-free until you make a withdrawal. What's more, you may be able to access this money when you purchase your first home or attend a post-secondary education program. (See the sections that talk about the RRSP Home Buyer's Plan and the Lifelong Learning Plan in Chapter 10.)

Spousal RRSPs

Spousal RRSPs allow couples to shift retirement income from one partner to the other—something that can help to reduce the amount of taxes they pay when they start taking money out of their RRSPs. Typically, the spouse with the higher income sets up a spousal RRSP in the name of the spouse with the lower income. The spouse with the higher income gets to deduct any spousal RRSP contributions from his or her taxes.

Spousal Tax Credit

This tax break, though small, is helpful for families in which one parent is at home raising the children. You can claim a credit of $915 if your partner earns less than $538 during the year (or a smaller credit if he or she earned between $538 and $5,820). If the spouse with the lower income earned slightly more than $5,820, he or she should make an RRSP contribution to bring his or her income down below the magic $5,820 mark, something that will entitle the higher income earner to a partial spousal credit.

Equivalent to Married Credit

If you are a single parent and support a relative who lives with you (e.g., your child), you can claim this credit. Revenue Canada rules state that the relative must be related to you, completely financially dependent on you, living in Canada, and (except in the case of a parent or grandparent) under the age of 18. Note: The age limit can be waived if you are responsible for a mentally or physically handicapped child over the age of 18.

the Bottom line

Tempted to file that tax return after April 30? Don't do it unless you're positive you're getting a refund. Revenue Canada charges a penalty of 5 percent of the tax owing plus an additional 1 percent for each month that you're late. That's not the whole story, however. You'll also be charged a hefty interest rate on your outstanding balance—the current T-bill rate plus 2 percent If you or your spouse are self-employed, the government allows you until June 15 to file your return, but any balance owing is due April 30. What a deal!

Canada Child Tax Benefit

If you are responsible for the care of a child who is under 18 years of age, you can apply for the Canada Child Tax Benefit (CCTB). You should fill out the necessary form—Form RC66 — Canada Child Tax Benefit Application—as soon as possible after your child's birth or adoption. Once the government processes your application, you will receive a notice indicating how much money you will receive. The CCTB is based on your income. The basic benefit is $1,020 per child, plus an additional $75 per child for third and subsequent children. You're also entitled to an additional $213 per child for whom no childcare expenses are claimed. The benefit is reduced by 5 percnet of your family's net income once your income creeps above $25,921. (Note: In single parent households, the benefit is reduced by 2.5 percent if your family's net income goes over this amount.) You are required to notify the government immediately if there is a change in your family's circumstances; for example, if your child is no longer living with you, you move, your marital status changes, or your banking information changes.

Childcare Expenses Deduction

If you and your partner work or attend school full-time, Revenue Canada allows you to deduct your childcare costs from your taxable income, to a maximum of $7,000 for each child who is seven or younger at the end of the year and $4,000 for each child who is between the age of seven and seventeen. In most parts of Canada, it is generally the spouse with the lower income who has to declare the childcare expenses on his or her tax return. (The exception is Quebec, where either partner is allowed to claim the deduction.) Your total childcare expense deduction can't, however, be more than two-thirds of your earned income (unless you happen to live in

Quebec, in which case you're allowed to claim up to 100 percent of the earned income of the spouse with the lower income). Note: If your spouse is a full-time student in a government-approved educational program, the spouse with the higher income can claim the childcare deduction.

"I do not believe that families with young children—especially those in which the mother is at home—get any significant or worthwhile tax breaks. The tax system is set up for the 'work more, gain more' mentality. Some tax breaks are given to offset daycare costs, but this is a ludicrous sham at best. And families living on only one income are not given any incentives in the form of a tax break. I would like to see a tax break for stay-at-home moms implemented in the near future."
— Fiona, 32, mother of six.

Spousal Support and Maintenance Payments Deduction

If you or your partner are responsible for making alimony or maintenance payments to a former partner, these payments may be tax deductible. While occasional lump-sum payments don't qualify, you can deduct regular, periodic payments that are made following a decree, order, judgement, or written agreement. Child support orders that were drawn up after April 30, 1997, are not tax deductible.

Moving Expenses Deduction

If you and your family move so that you or your partner can take a new job or start a new business, you can usually deduct the majority of your moving costs. You can deduct travelling costs (including meals and accommodations), moving company charges, mortgage penalties you incur by paying off your current mortgage early, storage costs, real estate commissions, legal fees, and other similar types of expenses. Similarly, students who relocate in order to study at a post-secondary institution are able to declare their moving expenses against any taxable scholarships, bursaries, research grants, or fellowships they receive. In order to declare your moving expenses, you have to move at least 40 kilometers closer to your new job or school.

Charitable Donations Tax Credit

If you and your partner regularly donate to charity, pool your tax receipts and declare them on one return. That way, you'll be able to take advantage of the higher charitable donation credits that kick in when you give more than $200 to charity in a single taxation year. If your contributions aren't enough to push you above the $200 level, hold on to your receipts and claim them every couple of years instead. Revenue Canada allows you to submit charitable donation receipts up to five years after the fact.

According to Revenue Canada, one in four Canadian taxpayers now files his or her tax return electronically.

Tuition fees

You can receive a credit worth 17 percent of tuition fees totalling $100 or more paid to a Canadian university, college, or other post-secondary institution during the taxation year. Tuition costs paid to a foreign university, college, or post-secondary institution may also qualify. You can also receive a $35-per-month educational status credit if you're a full-time student. Note: If a member of your family (perhaps your partner or your child) doesn't need the full tuition fee tax credit or the educational status credit to reduce his or her taxable income to zero, you can declare some or all of these credits on your tax return instead. Revenue Canada allows up to $850 of the unused portion of the tuition fee tax credit or the education tax credit to be transferred to a student's spouse, parent, or grandparent.

Medical expenses

If one or more members of your family have significant medical expenses over a twelve-month period (not over a single tax year), this is a tax credit you need to know about. You are allowed to deduct the portion of your medical expenses that exceed three percent of your net income. Eligible expenses include payments for medical or dental care, prescription drugs and medications, eyeglasses, treatment for speech or hearing problems, and the premiums for any private health insurance plans—including the cost of travel insurance you purchase when you're travelling outside of the country.

Note: If you or your spouse are self-employed, any health insurance premiums that you pay are fully tax-deductible.

The types of expenses covered by medical expense tax credits were significantly broadened in the 1997 budget. It's possible to obtain credits for

- 20 percent of the cost of a van that has been made wheelchair accessible (up to a maximum of $5,000)
- 50 percent of the cost of air conditioners for individuals suffering from certain diseases (e.g., chronic respiratory ailments), as opposed to the previous $1,000 maximum
- fees paid to a sign language interpreter
- the costs associated with moving to a wheelchair-accessible home
- the costs involved in widening a driveway to allow a mobility-impaired individual access to a bus
- part-time attendant care expenses of $10,000 per year (up from $5,000 in previous budgets), to $20,000 (up from $10,000 in previous budgets) if the individual died during the year

The government also introduced a tax credit for low-income Canadians with disabilities. The credit is for $500 or 25 percent of the allowable portion of medical expenses that can be claimed under the regular medical expense tax credit. Families with net incomes in excess of $16.069 don't, however, qualify for the full amount.

Disability credit

If your child or your partner suffers from a severe and prolonged mental or physical impairment, you are eligible for a $720 tax credit—$1,120 if your child is over the age of 18. The disability must be certified by a medical doctor or an optometrist (in the case of a visual impairment).

Self-employment expenses

If you or your partner run a business from your home, you are eligible to deduct a smorgasbord of business-related expenses: postage, office supplies, courier charges, office equipment, and more.

Don't wait for the folks at Revenue Canada to clue into the fact that you could be eligible for one or more of these deductions or credits. That's not how the tax game works here in Canada. Ask and you shall receive; forget to ask for what you're entitled to and you'll have to do without.

Twelve

The Next Generation

Four-year-old Katie may not be old enough to worry about mutual funds and tax breaks, but she's already mastered a concept that many adults have yet to grasp: you can't spend it if you don't have it.

According to a 1998 study by YTV Canada Inc., Canada's 2.4 million "tweens"—children aged nine to 14—have $1.5 billion of their own and their parents' money to spend each year.
Source: The Globe and Mail

Her mother, Melinda, 33, explains: "Katie decided that she wanted to buy a $30 bean bag chair. We told her that she would have to save half the money. She took the $5 that her Grandma gave her for Easter and earmarked it for her chair. This gave Grandma an opportunity to offer her a job helping with yardwork. After doing a few more jobs and cleaning all the coins out of the couch, she had enough money for her chair. We took her to the store and she bought it."

Three-year-old Timmy may be younger than Katie, but he's also becoming money-wise. His parents Heather, 32, and Gregory, 43, are teaching him important lessons in money management. "Timmy may only be three, but we're trying to teach him the value of money," Heather explains. "When he's buying something, we let him hand the money to the clerk and wait to get his change back. And when he receives any money, we take him to the bank so that he can deposit it."

Raising money-smart kids

Melinda and Heather aren't the only parents who are determined to equip their kids with money sense before they grow up and leave home. There's growing interest in this area and the financial services industry is listening.

According to journalist Julie Cazzin, who wrote about this trend in the *Maclean's Guide to Personal Finance 1999,* young investor programs are gaining popularity with the big banks: "All [of the big banks] have special no-fee children's accounts with interest rates higher than on adult accounts. And all now allow young savers to purchase Guaranteed Investment Certificates in small denominations—as little as $25."

According to Cazzin, the crème de la crème of children's money management programs is the one offered by the Bank of Montreal. It includes weekend workshops for kids and a snazzy board game called "The Simple Steps Investment Kit." More than 5,000 children have participated in the workshops and 40,000 board games have been distributed across the country. Clearly parents and educators are looking for ways to equip the next generation with the money skills needed to get by in an increasingly complex world.

Show Me the Money!

Want to encourage your child's teacher to put money management on the curriculum? Let her know about the Bank of Montreal's *My Money Investment Club.* The teachers' kit includes class lessons and a board game that covers the possible components of an investment portfolio (bank accounts, government bands, stocks, and mutual funds); the three basic asset classes (cash, fixed income, and equities); diversification; the important of starting a savings program early; and the rewards of charitable giving. Teachers can order a *My Money Investment* Club kit free of charge by calling 1-888-4JR-JAYS.

When—and how—to teach your kids about money

You know it's a good idea to teach kids about money; you might be surprised to learn, however, just how early their money management education should begin. Most experts agree that kids are able to grasp the concept of money by the time they reach the age of three.

Does this mean that you should have a heart-to-heart talk about the merits of various mutual funds? Of course not! What it means is that you should introduce the concept of money and give your child the chance to start handling small amounts of money on her own. It's important to explain in very simple terms what money is used for and why most of us aren't able to buy everything we want. Your child will probably want to know where the money comes from and how you get it when you need it.

Show Me the Money!

Make sure that your child understands that credit cards and debit cards are also a form of money. If a child doesn't see any cash changing hands, he or she might mistakenly conclude that you don't have to pay for items when you have a piece of plastic in your hand. (Hey, many adults make the same mistake!)

You should open up a savings account for your child by the time he or she turns ten so that she can begin to master the ins and outs of banking. If you're worried that her meagre savings will be eaten up by bank charges, have no fear. Most of the major chartered banks offer low-cost or no-cost savings accounts for children under the age of 18. Some are going a whole lot further, offering debit cards and guaranteed investment certificates in denominations of as little as $25, too. You should also encourage your 16-year-old to open up a chequing account. After all, there's an art to learning how to reconcile your account rather than succumbing to the temptation to spend on the basis of what is or isn't in there.

As your child gets a little older, be sure to include her in family discussions about money—especially those that involve setting financial goals. It's an approach that has worked well for Fiona, 32, and Christopher, 35, and their six children.

"We spend time talking with the kids about our financial goals and how we plan on achieving them," Fiona explains. "We strive to make these their goals as well so that they are part of the planning process. When they know why we are scrimping in some areas, they are more likely to be dedicated to saving and to come up with far fewer 'wants.' We also take them shopping so that they can see for themselves just how far a dollar doesn't go! Most importantly, we teach them that money is only a means to a far greater end—not an end in itself. Money is not where you want to go, only the means to get there."

Part of teaching your children to manage money is to arm them with the skills they need to become smart consumers. That means explaining how they can choose the cereal box size that offers the best value, demystifying TV commercials by pointing out how much less appetizing the real-life version of a fast food hamburger looks, and how much of a toy's on-air appeal is actually due to special effects.

The key, of course, is to avoid turning a learning opportunity into a mini-lecture. The messages heard and the lessons learned will be far more powerful if you allow the kids to draw their own conclusions. After all, you only have to buy a superhero figurine once to discover that it doesn't come with all of the neat accessories (or make any of the nifty noises!) that were demonstrated on TV.

Parents should to encourage their kids to make their own purchasing decisions and to budget for special purchases. This isn't always easy in a society that thrives on instant credit and instant gratification, says Vancouver-based parenting consultant Kathy Lynn. "If our kids are into instant gratification, it's for good reason," she insists. "It comes from not being asked to wait for anything. We need to teach them that if something's really worth having, it's worth waiting for."

Show Me the Money!

If your child is about to blow a month's allowance on a poorly made toy, you might want to offer your opinion—"That toy looks like it might break quite easily"—but that should be the extent of your involvement. If your child decides to go ahead with the purchase anyway and the toy subsequently breaks, resist the temptation to say, "I told you so," or to run out and replace the toy. Instead, demonstrate that you empathize with him and encourage him to return the broken toy to the store where it was purchased or to write a letter of complaint to the manufacturer or local newspaper.

Making allowances

Should children receive an allowance? Some parents say yes, and others says no.

Lori, 43, the mother of two teenagers, feels that giving her children an allowance helps them to learn how to manage their money. "My children get an allowance and have to live within those financial boundaries. Holding back or giving them less encourages them to look for a job or do extras around the house for spending money. I let them know that they need to work for money if they want nice things."

Lori is the first to admit that the money flowed a little too freely when her children were younger—something she regrets. "Don't buy your children everything they want," she advises. "They begin to think that you are a money tree and, believe me, they don't appreciate it. My children are older and I am continually cutting back on what I give them because there is no thanks and no appreciation. I am hoping that if I hold back long enough, lack of money will motivate them to get a part-time job."

Facts and Figures

Who's the boss? A study by Western International Media, a Los Angeles-based market research firm, indicated that 69 percent of American parents admit to giving into their children's whining and pleading for particular types of merchandise. The study found that 33 percent of video purchases and 40 percent of trips to such entertainment facilities as Discovery Zone, Chuck E. Cheese, and miniature golf courses occur because the child requests it. Even worse, an earlier study conducted by the same company found that 46 percent of toys would not have been bought had the child not nagged his or her parents into making the purchase.

Leigh, 31, and Thomas, 32, the parents of two young children, also think it's beneficial to give children an allowance: "Our six-year-old gets an allowance of four dollars per week. That may sound like a lot, but out of that she's expected to contribute money to her Sunday school envelope and pay her dues for Beavers. This leaves her with about two dollars a week for spending money. The money she receives isn't tied to household responsibilities: I don't get paid for making my bed!"

Fiona and Christopher take a different approach when it comes to providing their six children with spending money. "We do not give our children an allowance," Fiona explains. "They are expected to help with chores and responsibilities around the house because they live here. We buy their clothes, shoes, coats, etc., and on occasion give them money to blow on treats or whatever else they may want. Even kids need a little 'mad money' once in a while."

If you do decide to go the allowance route, you should plan to review the amount of each child's allowance once each year—perhaps at the beginning or end of the school year—and to move it upward if he or she is ready to assume responsibility for a wider range of purposes (e.g., junk food, entertainment expenses, clothing, and so on). If your child wants a larger increase than you initially offer, ask her to prove to you that she's ready for the added financial responsibility. If she makes a convincing case, rethink your position. Perhaps she really is ready to move to the front of the class.

Money Talk

"Blessed are the young, for they shall inherit the national debt."
– U.S President Herbert Hoover

Conclusion

"Children are poor men's riches."
- English Proverb.

We've covered a lot of ground over the last 12 Chapters. We've talked about how having children changes your financial priorities overnight—for better and for worse—and how tough it can be to make your paycheque stretch far enough to cover all the financial demands you face during this wonderful but crazy stage of your life.

I hope you've learned a lot from this book. I know I certainly have. In fact, I'm going to let you in on a secret: the money I will make on this book will be a mere fraction of the money my family and I will save as a result of the assorted bits of wisdom that I picked up while researching and writing it. (I'd prefer that you didn't pass that particular piece of information on to my publisher. The chief number-cruncher might decide to cancel my royalty payments, figuring that I've already made enough money on this particular book.)

I'd love to hear your comments on the book—good, bad, and ugly. (Actually, don't bother with the ugly!) You can either write to me care of my publisher at the address below or you can reach me via e-mail at pageone@kawartha.com

In the meantime, thanks for joining me for this ride through the weird and wonderful world of family finance.

Ann Douglas
Author, *Family Finance*
c/o Prentice Hall Canada Inc.
23 Prince Andrew Place
P.O. Box 580
Don Mills, Ontario
M3C 2T8

Appendix A: Glossary

Having difficulty decoding your life insurance policy or making sense of your mortgage agreement? You've come to the right place. You'll find concise definitions of key financial terms—something that should help to demystify any document that the financial industry chooses to throw your way. (Well, maybe!)

Administrator The person appointed by the court to represent an estate when no will was provided or the will does not name an executor. This person is sometimes referred to as a *personal representative* or *estate trustee without a will*.

Amortization period The number of years it will take to fully repay your mortgage.

Annuity An investment that pays you a fixed amount of money for a specified number of years or for life.

Appraised value An estimate of the market value of a property.

Appreciated or appreciating asset An asset whose value has increased or continues to increase due to a variety of factors, including inflation.

Assets Things you own, including your house, car, or investments.

Beneficiary A person who has been chosen to receive income or assets under the terms of a will, trust, or other type of policy or investment.

Blended payment A mortgage payment that consists of both principal and interest payments. The principal portion increases each month and the interest portion decreases, but the total monthly payment stays the same.

Bonds A type of investment that is offered by governments and corporations. You lend a sum of money to the issuer for a set amount of time at a fixed rate of interest.

Canada Mortgage and Housing Corporation (CMHC) A Crown corporation that administers the National Housing Act for the federal government and creates and sells mortgage loan insurance products.

Canada Education Savings Grant An educational savings grant that is paid by the federal government. The government tops up contributions made to an RESP by 20 percent up to a yearly maximum of $400 per beneficiary.

Capital property Assets such as shares, bonds, and real estate that you hold as an investment.

Capital gain or loss The difference between the price you paid for an investment and the price at which you sell it—in other words, the profit or loss you make.

Cash value insurance Life insurance that contains a savings account along with coverage for the life of the insured.

Certified Financial Planner (CFP) A financial planner who has met the training and testing requirements of the Financial Planners Standards Council of Canada or the Canadian Institute of Financial Planning.

Closed mortgage A mortgage agreement that cannot be prepaid, renegotiated or refinanced before maturity without paying a penalty.

Closing date The date on which the sale of property becomes final and the new owner takes possession.

Codicil A written and properly witnessed legal change or amendment to a will.

Collateral mortgage A loan that is backed by a promissory note and the security of a mortgage on a property.

Collateral Assets that are pledged by a borrower as security for repayment of a loan or other debt.

Community property A term that is used to describe the assets and property acquired after marriage that are owned equally by marriage partners. Also known as *family property*.

Compound interest Interest that is paid on interest. This occurs when interest is paid on an investment at periodic intervals and then added to the amount of the investment.

Conditional offer An offer to buy a property if certain conditions are met (for example, a satisfactory appraisal).

Condominium When individuals own apartments in a building or complex, but common areas are shared with other owners.

Consumer price index (CPI) A measure of the annual increase in the cost of certain consumer goods and services, which is used as a common indicator of inflation.

Contribution The amount of money you put into a savings/investment plan.

Conventional mortgage A mortgage that does not exceed 75 percent of the appraised value or purchase price of the property, whichever is less. Mortgage loan insurance is not required for this type of mortgage.

Current yield The annual rate of return on an investment expressed as a percentage.

Current return The annual return on an investment expressed in dollars.

Deferred profit sharing plan (DPSP) A vehicle that is used for saving for retirement. It offers certain tax advantages to the employer and any income earned in the plan accumulates tax-free as long as the funds remain in the plan.

Dividends Company earnings that are paid out to shareholders. Dividends can be earned on stocks and certain mutual funds.

Domicile A person's fixed place of residence.

Effective interest rate The real rate of interest after the effects of compounding are factored in.

Estate trustee without a will See *Administrator*.

Estate planning The process of planning for the orderly transfer of all your assets to heirs and others in a manner calculated to minimize taxes, expenses, and delays.

Executor The person or institution named in a will to carry out its provisions and instructions. Also known as a personal representative or estate trustee.

Family property A term that is used to describe the assets and property acquired after marriage that are owned equally by marriage partners. Also known as *community property*.

Financial advisors The team of experts you use to help you make investment decisions. These could include a lawyer, a chartered accountant, a financial planner, a banker, and/or a stockbroker.

Firm offer An offer to buy a particular property, as outlined in the offer to purchase, that has no conditions attached.

Fixed rate mortgage A mortgage for which the rate of interest is fixed for a specific period of time (the term).

Floating rate mortgage See *Variable rate mortgage*.

Foreclosure A legal procedure in which the lender obtains ownership of the property after the borrower has defaulted on payment.

Grantor The person who establishes or creates a trust. Also called a *settlor*.

Gross debt-service (GDS) ratio The percentage of gross income required to cover monthly payments associated with housing. Most lenders recommend that the GDS ratio be no more than 32 percent of your gross monthly income.

Guaranteed investment certificate (GIC) An investment in which you deposit money over a fixed period of time and are paid a set rate of interest.

Guardian A person who is legally responsible for managing the affairs and the care of a minor or incompetent person.

Healthcare power of attorney A document that gives someone authority to make medical or personal-care decisions for the person executing it.

Heir A person who is legally entitled to receive another person's property through inheritance.

High-ratio mortgage A mortgage in which you have less than a 25 percent down payment. By law, your mortgage must be insured against payment default to a certain maximum through either CMHC or an approved private insurer.

Income tax Federal and provincial tax that is paid on any income you receive.

Income deferral Postponing income until a future year in order to delay paying taxes on it.

Income-splitting A financial strategy that involves shifting income from the hands of one family member to another. It can help to reduce your family's overall tax burden.

Informal trust Also known as an in-trust account, this is an investment account that is registered in an adult's name but used to save/invest funds for a child.

Inheritance tax A tax that is levied on inherited property in some U.S. states. Tax rates typically depend on the relationship of the heir to the deceased. There are no inheritance taxes in Canada.

Interest The money you earn on an investment or pay on a loan.

Intestate Dying without a will.

Investment Something you put your money into in order to make money.

Investment income Money that is earned on investments you make. Investment income includes interest, dividends, and capital gains.

Irrevocable trust A trust that cannot be changed or cancelled. The opposite of a revocable trust.

Joint tenancy A form of property ownership in which one partner inherits the property in the event of the death of the other.

Leverage The use of borrowed money to acquire investment assets.

Liabilities The amount of money you owe to various creditors.

Lien The mortgage lender's legal claim to the borrower's property.

Liquidity This term describes your ability to respond quickly to an immediate need for cash. It usually involves having Canada Savings Bonds or other investments that are easily converted to cash.

Living trust A revocable or irrevocable written agreement into which a living person transfers assets and property along with instructions to a trustee, who then manages them and plans for their future distribution.

Maturity date Last day of the term of an investment or loan.

Mortgage life insurance Insurance on the outstanding balance of your mortgage.

Mutual funds An investment product in which your money is pooled with the money of many other investors. When you invest in a mutual fund, you purchase units of that fund.

Net worth Your total assets less your total liabilities.

Open mortgage A mortgage in which you can repay the loan, in part or in full, at any time prior to maturity without penalty.

Personal representative See *Administrator*.

Portfolio A collection of investments.

Power of attorney for property A legal document that gives another person full legal authority to handle property-related and/or financial matters. It can be general-purpose or a restricted power to deal with financial matters.

Preapproved mortgage Preliminary approval by the lender of the borrower's application for a mortgage to a certain maximum amount and rate.

Prepayment charge A fee that is charged by the lender when the borrower prepays all or part of a closed mortgage more quickly than is stated in the mortgage agreement.

Prenuptial agreement A contract agreed to by a couple prior to marriage that defines rights upon death or divorce.

Principal The amount of money that was originally borrowed.

Probate court A specialized court in each province that is set up to handle the management of wills, estates of persons dying without a will, and other related functions, such as guardianships.

Refinance To pay in full and discharge a mortgage and then arrange for a new mortgage with the same or a different lender.

Registered Educational Savings Plan (RESP) A tax-sheltered plan that is designed to help parents and grandparents accumulate funds for the post-secondary education costs of children or grandchildren.

Registered Retirement Savings Plan (RRSP) A plan that allows you to save for your retirement. Contributions are tax deductible and the funds within the plan grow tax-free until they are withdrawn.

Registered Pension Plan (RPP) A pension plan that is sponsored by your employer.

Registered Retirement Income Fund (RRIF) A fund that can be established with the proceeds of a maturing RRSP to provide retirement income.

Return The income earned and/or capital gain realized on an investment.

Risk The probability of loss in the future.

Second mortgage A mortgage that is granted when there is already a mortgage registered against the property.

Security In the case of mortgages, property that is offered in order to back a loan.

Segregated funds A type of mutual fund that provides a guarantee of the capital invested over a period of time.

Separate property Property owned only by one marriage partner that is kept segregated from the couple's family property.

Settlor The person who establishes or creates a trust. Also called a *grantor*.

Stocks Publicly-traded shares in a company.

Surtax An additional income tax over and above the regular income tax amount.

Tax credits Credits that reduce the amount of tax that you have to pay.

Tax bracket The rate of income tax you pay.

Tax shelter An investment that features significant tax savings, such as immediate deductions, credits, or income deferral.

Term The length of time a mortgage agreement covers.

Term deposit An investment product in which you deposit a fixed sum of money for a set period of time and are paid interest.

Term insurance Insurance that provides protection for a specific term or time period, with no investment component.

Testamentary trust A trust that is created by the deceased's will. Most wills include this provision for minors' interest.

Total debt-service (TDS) ratio The percentage of your gross income that is needed to cover monthly payments for housing and all other debts and financing obligations. It should not exceed 40 percent of your gross monthly income.

Treasury bill Short-term government debt that does not pay interest but is sold at discount and matures at its full face value.

Trust agreement A document that sets out instructions for managing the property left in a living trust, including who is to receive each portion of the trust assets.

Trust A written and formal agreement that enables a person or institution to hold property and manage it for the benefit of the beneficiaries.

Trustee The person or institution that is given the authority to manage trust property according to the instructions contained in the trust agreement.

Umbrella coverage Insurance coverage over and above the liability limits of other specific insurance policies.

Variable-rate mortgage A mortgage with a rate of interest that changes as money market conditions change. The regular payments stay the same for a specific period. However, the amount applied toward the principal changes according to the movement of interest rates. Also referred to as a *floating rate mortgage*.

Vendor-take-back A mortgage in which the vendor (seller) of a property provides some or all of the mortgage financing in order to sell the property.

Will A document that provides for the transfer of your estate to your beneficiaries and that appoints a guardian to care for any minor children.

Appendix B: Directory of Canadian Financial Organizations

Chartered banks

Bank of Montreal
129 rue St. Jacques
Montreal, Quebec
H2Y 1L6
Tel: 514-877-7373
Web: www.bmo.com

The Bank of Nova Scotia
44 King Street West
Toronto, Ontario
M5H 1H1
Tel: 416-866-6161
Web: www.scotiabank.ca

Canadian Imperial Bank of Commerce
Commerce Court
Toronto, Ontario
M5L 1A2
Tel: 416-980-2211
Web: www.cibc.com

Canadian Western Bank
2300-10303 Jasper Avenue
Edmonton, Alberta
T5J 3X6
Tel: 403-423-8888
Web: http://cwbank.com

Citizens Bank of Canada
Box 13133, Station Terminal
Vancouver, British Columbia
V6B 6K1
Tel: 604-708-7800

Web: **www.citizens.com**
First Nations Bank of Canada
224 Fourth Avenue South
Saskatoon, Saskatchewan
S7K 5M5
Tel: 1-888-454-3622

Laurentian Bank of Canada
1981 McGill College Avenue
Montreal, Quebec
H3A 3K3
Tel: 514-522-1846
Web: **www.laurentianbank.com**

Manulife Bank of Canada
500 King Street
Waterloo, Ontario
N2J 4C6
Tel: 1-800-MANULIFE
     519-747-1700;
Web: **www.manulife.com**

National Bank of Canada
600 de la Gauchetiere West
Montreal, Quebec
H3B 4L2
Tel: 514-394-4000
Web: **www.nbc.ca**

Royal Bank of Canada
P.O. Box 6001
Montreal, Quebec
H3C 3A9
Tel: 514-874-2110
Web: **www.royalbank.com**

Toronto Dominion Bank
P.O. Box I
Toronto Dominion Centre
Toronto, Ontario
M5K IA2
Tel: 416-982-8222
Web: **www.tdbank.ca**

Credit counselling agencies (not for profit)

British Columbia
Credit Counselling Society of British Columbia
Toll Free: 1-888-527-8999 (only in BC)
Tel: 604-527-8999; Fax: 604-527-8008

Debtors Assistance Branch
Ministry of Attorney General
Toll free: 1-800-663-7867 (only in BC)
Victoria: Tel: 250-387-1747; Fax: 250-953-4783
Burnaby: Tel: 604-660-3550; Fax: 604-660-8472
Kamloops: Tel: 250-828-4511; Fax: 250-371-3822

Alberta
Credit Counselling Services of Alberta
Toll free: 1-888-294-0076 (only in Alberta)
Calgary: Tel: 403-265-2201; Fax: 403-265-2240
Edmonton: Tel: 403-423-5265; Fax: 403-423-2791

Saskatchewan
Department of Justice, Provincial Mediation Board
Regina: Tel: 306-787-5387; Fax: 306-787-5574
Saskatoon: Tel: 306-933-6520; Fax: 306-933-7030

Manitoba
Community Financial Counselling Services
Tel: 204-989-1900, Fax: 204-989-1908

Ontario
Ontario Association of Credit Counselling Services
Tel: 1-888-7IN DEBT (746-3328) Fax: 905-945-4680

Quebec

Fédération des associations cooperatives d'économique familiale du Québec
Tel: 514-271-7004; Fax: 514-271-1036

Option-consommateurs
Tel: 514-598-7288; Fax: 514-598-8511

Newfoundland and Labrador

Personal Credit Counselling Services
Tel: 709-753-5812; Fax: 709-753-3390

Prince Edward Island

Department of Community Affairs
Consumer, Corporate and Insurance Services
Tel: 902-368-4580; Fax: 902-368-5355

Nova Scotia

Port Cities Debt Counselling Society
Tel: 902-453-6510

Access Nova Scotia
Department of Business and Consumer Services
Tel: 1-800-670-4357 (only in Nova Scotia); Fax: 902-424-0720

New Brunswick

Credit Counselling Services of Atlantic Canada, Inc.
Toll Free: 1-800-539-2227 (only in New Brunswick)
Tel: 506-652-1613; Fax: 506-633-6057

Consumer Services Officer
Consumer Affairs Branch, Department of Justice
Tel: 506-453-2659; Fax 506-444-4494

Family Services of Fredericton Inc.
Tel: 506-458-8211; Fax: 506-451-9437

Yukon

Contact Consumer Services for referral
Tel: 867-667-5111; Fax: 867-667-3609

Northwest Territories

Consumer Services
Municipal and Community Affairs
Tel: 867-873-7125; Fax: 867-920-6343

Miscellanous financial organizations

Associated Credit Bureaus of Canada
80 Bloor Street W., Suite 900
Toronto, Ontario
M5S 2V1
Tel: 416-969-2247

Bank of Canada
234 Wellington Street
Ottawa, Ontario
K1A 0G9
Tel: 1-800-303-1282
Fax: 613-782-7713
Web: **www.bank-banque-canada.ca**
E-mail: paffairs@bank-banque-canada.ca

Business Development Bank of Canada (BDC)
5 Place Ville Marie, 4th Floor
Montreal, Quebec
H3B 5E7
Tel: 1-888-463-6232
(Regional Office numbers listed in the blue pages (federal
government section)
Web: **www.bdc.ca**

Canada Deposit Insurance Corporation
50 O'Connor Street, 17th Floor
P.O. Box 2340, Station D
Ottawa, Ontario
K1P 5W5
Tel: 1-800-461-2342
Web: **www.cdic.ca**

Canada Mortgage and Housing Corporation
700 Montreal Road
Ottawa, Ontario
K1A 0P7
Tel: 1-800-668-2642
     613-748-2000
Fax: 613-748-2098
Web: **www.cmhc-schl.gc.ca**
E-mail: chic@cmhc-schl.gc.ca

Canadian Association of Financial Planners
439 University Avenue, Suite 1710
Toronto, Ontario
M5G 1Y8
Tel: 1-800-346-2237
     416-593-6592
Web: **www.cafp.org**

Canadian Bankers Association
P.O. Box 348
Commerce Court West,
199 Bay Street, 30th Floor,
Toronto, Ontario
M5L 1G2
Tel: 416-362-6092
Web: **www.cba.ca**

Canadian Depository for Securities Limited
85 Richmond Street West
Toronto, Ontario
M5H 2C9
Tel: 416-365-8400
Web: **www.cds.ca**

Canadian Life and Health Insurance Association Inc.
Consumer Assistance Centre
1 Queen Street East
Suite 1700
Toronto, Ontario.
M5C 2X9
Tel: 1-800-268-8099
     416-777-2344
Web: **www.clhia.ca**

Canadian Payments Association
1212-50 O'Connor Street
Ottawa, Ontario
K1P 6L2
Tel: 613-238-4173
Fax: 613-233-3385
Web: **www.cdnpay.ca**

Canadian Real Estate Association
344 Slater Street, Suite 1600
Ottawa, Ontario
K1R 7Y3
Tel: 613-237-7111
Web: **http://realtors.mls.ca/crea/**

Canadian Securities Institute
121 King Street W. Suite 1550
P.O. Box 113
Toronto, Ontairo
M5H 3T9
Tel: 1-800-274-8355
    416-364-9130
Fax: 416-359-0486
Web: **www.csi.ca**

Canadian Tax Foundation
595 Bay Street, Suite 1200
Toronto, Ontario
M5G 2N5
Tel: 416-599-0283
Web: **www.ctf.ca**

Consumers Association of Canada
267 O'Connor Street, Suite 307
Ottawa, Ontario
K2P IV3
Tel: 613-238-2533
Web: **www.consumer.ca**

Credit Institute of Canada
5090 Explorer Drive, Suite 501
Mississauga, Ontario
L4W 3T9
Tel: 905-629-9805
Web: www.credit.edu.org

Consultations & Communications Branch
Finance Canada
L'Esplanade Laurier
140 O'Connor Street
Ottawa, Ontario
K1A 0G5
Tel: 613-992-1573
Web: **www.fin.gc.ca**

Equifax Canada Inc.
60 Bloor Street West, Suite 1200
Toronto, Ontario
M4W 3C1
Tel: 1-800-361-4430

Export Development Corporation (EDC)
151 O'Connor Street
Ottawa, Ontario
K1A 1K3
Tel: 1-800-267-8510
    613-598-2500
Fax: 613-598-6697
Web: **www.edc.ca**
E-mail: export@edc4.edc.ca

Industry Canada
235 Queen Street
Ottawa, Ontario
K1A 0H5
Tel: 613-954-2788
Fax: 613-954-1894;
Web: **http://info.ic.gc.ca**

The Institute of Canadian Bankers
Scotia Tower, Suite 1000
1002 Sherbrooke Street West
Montreal, Quebec
H3A 3M5
Tel: 1-800-361-4636
    514-282-9480
Fax: 514-282-2881
Web: **http://icb.org**

Insurance Bureau of Canada
151 Yonge Street, 18th Floor
Toronto, Ontario
M5C 2W7
Tel: 1-800-387-2880
     416-362-2031
Web: www.ibc.ca

Insurance Institute of Canada
18 King Street East, 6th Floor
Toronto, Ontario
M5C 1C4
Tel: 416-362-8586
Web: http://iic-iac.org

Interac Association
P.O. Box 109
121 King Street West, Suite 1905
Toronto, Ontario
M5H 3T9
Tel: 416-362-8550
Fax: 416-869-5080
Web: http://interac.org

Investment Dealers Association of Canada
121 King Street W. Suite 1600
Toronto, Ontario
M5H 3T9
Tel: 416-364-6133

The Investment Funds Institute of Canada
151 Yonge Street, 5th Floor
Toronto, Ontario
M5C 2W7
Tel: 1-888-865-4232
     416-363-2158
Fax: 416-861-9937
Web: www.mutfunds.com/ific

Investors Association of Canada
26 Soho Street, Suite 380
Toronto, Ontario
M5T 1Z7
Tel: 416-340-1722
Web: www.iac.ca

Office of the Superintendent of Financial Institutions
255 Albert Street
Ottawa, Ontario
K1A 0H2
Tel: 1-800-385-8647
     613-990-7788
Web: www.osfi-bsif.gc.ca

Quebec Deposit Insurance Board
800 place d'Youville
Quebec City, Quebec
G1R 4Y5
Tel: 1-800-463-5662
     418-528-9728
Web: http://igif.gouv.qc.ca

Royal Canadian Mint
320 Sussex Drive
Ottawa, Ontario
K1A 0G8
Tel: 1-800-267-1871
Web: http://rcmint.ca

Statistics Canada
Tunney's Pasture
Ottawa, Ontario
K1A 0T6
Tel: 1-800-263-1136
Web: www.statcan.ca

Appendix C: Web Site Directory

Web site	Highlights

Banking

Canadian Bankers Association - Publications
www.cba.ca/eng/Publications/pubs_index.htm

Drop by this page of the Canadian Bankers Association site to order your copies of some of the many excellent booklets available to consumers. Topics include mortgages, managing credit, and much more. (If you don't have Internet access, call 1-800-263-0231 instead.)

Canada Deposit Insurance Corporation
www.cdic.ca/english/members/dir.htm

Trying to find the Web site of a Canadian financial institution? Have I got a Web page for you. You'll find the big banks as well as ones you've never even heard of, like the Mellon Bank of Canada. You can find detailed information about the CDIC elsewhere on the same site.

Industry Canada's Office of Consumer Affairs
strategis.ic.gc.ca/sc_consu/consaffairs/engdoc/oca.html

Contains a number of useful tools, including a financial service charges calculator that allows you to compare the monthly service charge packages of various financial institutions and the credit card costs calculator that can help you decide which credit card is right for you.

Family finance

"Budgeting for baby," Women's Wire
www.womenswire.com/basics/babybud get.html

While the article is intended for American parents, it still has lots of valuable information for Canadian parents—like how not to go totally bankrupt when shopping for baby.

"Life Events: Parenting," Quicken.com
www.quicken.com

> The U.S. counterpart to Quicken.ca, Quicken.com devotes an entire section of its Web site to the financial fall-out of becoming a parent. Definitely worth a visit.

"Family Finance," Sanity Savers.com
www.sanitysavers.com/familyfinance.htm

> The official Web site for this book. You'll find articles and links of interest to families with young children.

"Two For The Money," MSNBC
www.msnbc.com/news/158247.asp

> A provocative article that asks the question, "Will a second income end up actually costing your family cash?"

There's Something About Money
www.yourmoney.cba.ca/

> The Canadian Bankers' Association's newly launched Web site for kids. Both cool and informative!

Financial information in general

Sympatico
www1.sympatico.ca/Tools/tools.html

> You'll find all kinds of nifty tools on this page, both financial and nonfinancial: a car lease calculator, currency converters, fund quotes, online trading, credit card rates, mortgage rates, and much more. While you're in the neighbourhood, check out the Personal Finance Calculators page, too: **www1.sympatico.ca/Contents/Finance/calculators.html**

iMoney
www.imoney.com/timely/rates/credit_card.html

> The easiest way to find out the interest rates and fees associated with various credit cards.

CANNEX Com
www.cannex.com/canada

> The place to go for information on interest rates, unit values, and product information for annuities, term deposits, guaranteed investment certificates, mortgages, registered term deposits, RRSPs, deposit accounts, and RRIFs.

Quicken.ca
www.quicken.ca/eng/home/index.html

> One of the best personal finance Web sites out there. You'll find interesting articles, tools and calculators galore, and practical how-to guides on a range of financial topics. There's also a Small Business Centre that's packed with useful information for anyone who's thinking of hanging out their own shingle.

CANOE Money
www.canoe.ca/planner/home.html

> Wondering how financially fit your family is? This online tool will help you decide.

IE:Money
www.iemoney.com

> This is the Web site of the Canadian personal finance magazine of the same name. You'll find a sampling of articles from the current issue as well as past issues of the magazine.

Home buying

Canada Mortgage
www.canadamortgage.com/stats

> If you love high-tech bells and whistles such as multi-coloured graphs, you'll love this site. It's packed with valuable information you won't find anywhere else—like a graph that shows how the one-year mortgage rate has fared over the past 20 years.

Canada Mortgage and Housing Corporation
www.cmhc-schl-gc.ca

> Everything you ever wanted to know about CMHC—but were too confused to ask. Be sure to download your free copy of *Homebuying Step-by-Step,* an excellent guide to the ins and outs of purchasing a home.

Insurance

Canadian Life and Health Insurance Association Inc.
www.clhia.ca

> An excellent source of information on the Canadian insurance industry. There's also an extensive list of publications of interest to consumers, many of which are free.

Life Underwriters Association of Canada
www.luac.com

> Contains interesting facts about the life insurance industry in Canada.

HealthyWay
healthcentral.sympatico.ca/LifeView/html/intro.html

> Wondering how long you can expect to live, given your family history and your lifestyle habits? Complete the LifeView® lifestyle profile at this site and find out for yourself.

Taxes

Revenue Canada
www.rc.gc.ca

> It may not be the friendliest of Web sites, but it's certainly got every form, guide, or interpretation bulletin you could ever need. There are also FAQs galore, in case you, like the rest of us, are having a little difficulty making sense of the Canadian Income Tax Act.

Note: You'll also want to check out the Web sites that are listed in the Directory of Organizations in Appendix B.

Appendix D : Recommended Readings

Books

Carroll, Jim, CA, and Rick Broadhead, MBA. *Canadian Money Management Online.* Scarborough: Prentice Hall Canada Inc., 1996.

Douglas, Ann. *The Unofficial Guide to Childcare.* New York: Macmillan, Inc., 1998.

Douglas, Ann. *The Unofficial Guide to Having A Baby.* New York: Macmillan, Inc., 1999.

Estess, Patricia Schiff, and Irving Barocas. *Kids, Money & Values.* Cincinnati: Betterway Books, 1994.

Fields, Denise, and Alan Fields. *Baby Bargains.* Boulder: Windsor Peak Press, 1997.

Fisher, Sarah Young, and Carol Turkington. *Everything You Need to Know About Money and Investing.* Paramus, NJ: Prentice Hall Press, 1998.

Ginsberg, Laurence. *The Complete Idiot's Guide to Being an Entrepreneur in Canada,* Revised. Scarborough: Prentice Hall Canada Inc., 1999.

Heady, Robert K., Christy Heady, and Bruce McDougall. *The Complete Idiot's Guide to Managing Your Money in Canada.* Scarborough: Prentice Hall Canada Inc., 1998.

Hetzer, Barbara. *How Can I Ever Afford Children. Money Skills for New and Experienced Parents.* New York: John Wiley & Sons, Inc., 1998.

Homebuying Step By Step. A Consumer Guide and Workbook. Ottawa: Canada Mortgage and Housing Corporation, 1998.

Lavine, Alan, Gail Liberman, and Stephen Nelson. *The Complete Idiot's Guide to Making Money with Mutual Funds for Canadians.* Scarborough: Prentice Hall Canada Inc., 1998.

Lawrence, Judy. *The Budget Kit. The Common Cents Money Management Workbook.* Chicago: Dearborn Financial Publishing Inc., 1997.

Lipper, Ari, and Joanna Lipper. *Baby Stuff.* New York: Dell Publishing, 1997.

Maple, Steve, and Edward Olkovich. *The Complete Idiot's Guide to Wills and Estates for Canadians.* Scarborough: Prentice Hall Canada Inc., 1998.

McDougall, Bruce. *The Complete Idiot's Guide to Personal Finance for Canadians.* Scarborough: Prentice Hall Canada Inc., 1998.

McDougall, Bruce, and Shelley O'Hara. *The Complete Idiot's Guide to Buying and Selling a Home in Canada.* Scarborough: Prentice Hall Canada Inc., 1997.

Mosbacher, Georgette. *It Takes Money, Honey.* New York: HarperCollins Publishers, Inc., 1999.

Pape, Gordon, and Frank Jones. *Head Start. How to Save for Your Children's or Grandchildren's Education.* Toronto: Stoddart Publishing Company Limited, 1998.

Pape, Gordon, with Bruce McDougall. *The Canadian Mortgage Book.* Scarborough: Prentice Hall Canada Inc., 1997.

Rafelman, Rachel. *Baby Gear for the First Year.* Toronto: Macmillan Canada, 1997.

Sandler, Corey. *Secrets of the Savvy Consumer.* Paramus, NJ: Prentice Hall, 1998.

Seed, Nicholas, Danielle Lacasse, Anne Jewett, and Irene Jacob. *Deloitte & Touche—Canadian Guide to Personal Financial Management.* Scarborough: Prentice Hall Canada Inc., 1999.

Skousen, Mark, and Jo Ann Skousen. *High Finance on a Low Budget.* Chicago: Dearborn Financial Publishing, Inc., 1997.

The Maclean's Guide To Personal Finance 1999. Toronto: Maclean Hunter Publishing Limited, 1998.

Tyson, Eric, and Tony Martin. *Personal Finance for Dummies for Canadians.* Foster City, CA: IDG Books Worldwide, Inc., 1998.

From the Kitchen Table to the Boardroom Table. Nepean: The Vanier Institute of the Family, 1998.

The Manager's Work-Family Toolkit. Nepean: The Vanier Institute of the Family, 1998.

Wyatt, Elaine. *The Money Companion.* Scarborough: ITP Nelson, 1999.

Yaccato, Joanne Thomas. *Balancing Act: A Canadian Woman's Financial Success Guide,* Revised and Updated. Scarborough: Prentice Hall Canada Inc., 1999.

Booklets

Note: All of theses booklets are by the Canadian Bankers Association and are available upon request. Call 1–800–263–0231.

Canadian Bank Facts 97-98. Toronto: Canadian Bankers Association, 1998.

Commerce Enters a New Age. Toronto: Canadian Bankers Association, 1998.

Getting Started in Small Business. Toronto: Canadian Bankers Association, 1998.

Helping You Bank—An Introduction. Toronto: Canadian Bankers Association, 1998.

Investing Your Dollars. Toronto: Canadian Bankers Association, 1998.

Managing Money. Toronto: Canadian Bankers Association, 1998.

Mortgage Wise. Toronto: Canadian Bankers Association, 1998.

Planning for Retirement. Toronto: Canadian Bankers Association, 1998.

Preparing Business For The Year 2000. Toronto: Canadian Bankers Association, 1998.

Safeguarding Your Interests. Toronto: Canadian Bankers Association, 1998.

Saving for Your Children's Education. Toronto: Canadian Bankers Association, 1998.

The Economy and You. Toronto: Canadian Bankers Association, 1998.

The Interest in Your Life. Toronto: Canadian Bankers Association, 1998.

Newspaper, magazine, and online articles

Allentuck, Andrew. "Credit Cards: Know When To Fold 'Em." *The Globe and Mail,* 23 February, 1999: R4.

Barros, Jennifer. "Winning The Grocery Game: How A Family Of Seven Eats For Less Than $50 a Week." *Mother Earth News,* 18 August, 1998: 14(2).

Bell, Kevin. "Living The Frugal Life—Miser's Simpler Lifestyle Leads to Financial Independence." *The Ottawa Sun,* 24 January, 1999: 30.

Belsky, Gary. "Stop Throwing Away $5,000 a Year if You Use Our 27 Tips to Spend Less on Your Home, Car, Insurance and More, You Can Live Better Than Ever." *Money,* January 1, 1997: 122.

Bettencourt, Michael. "A Site for Money Savers." *The Toronto Star,* 22 August, 1998.

Biscott, Lynn. "Many Happy Returns—Basic Tax Strategies." *The Globe and Mail,* 9 April, 1996: C2.

Bourette, Susan. "25% Plan to Buy Home in 2 Years: Survey." *The Globe and Mail,* 27 January, 1999: B6.

Buckstein, Jeff. "Answers From Financial Pros." *The Globe and Mail,* 9 April, 1996: C1.

Buckstein, Jeff. "Self-Employed Create Own Benefits." *The Globe and Mail,* 23 February, 1999: R3.

Caplin, Joan. "One Family's Finances: Bickering Over Bucks. She's a Spender, and He's a Saver. Sparks Fly Constantly. After 15 Years of

Fighting Over Money They Are Just Beginning to Learn to Compromise." *Money*, 1 January, 1996: 90.

Carrick, Rob. "A Rough Guide to RRSPs on the Web." *The Globe and Mail*, 30 January, 1999: B7.

Carrick, Rob. "Condescension Clouds Attitude to Investing Public." *The Globe and Mail*, 27 April, 1999: B18.

Cestnick, Tim. "A Little Co-operation with Ex Can Pay Off." *The Globe and Mail*, 23 February, 1999: R2.

Chisholm, Patricia, with Sharon Doyle Driedger, Susan McClelland, and Brian Bergman. "The Mother Load: Superwoman Is Burned out. Should Mom Stay Home?" *Maclean's*, 1 March, 1999: 46.

Cohen, Bruce, "Rule Changes Add to RESP Allure." *The Globe and Mail*, 2 December, 1998. C1.

Cohen, Bruce. "Helping Hands for the Third Generation." *The Globe & Mail*, 2 December, 1998: C2.

Crenshaw, Albert B. "Marital Money: To Merge or Not to Merge?" *Newsday*, 1 June, 1997: F09.

Cross, L.D. "Family Finance—John And Jean Canuck." *The Financial Post Magazine*, January 1999: 71.

Espinoza, Galina. "Who's the Money Boss in Your Family?" *Working Mother*, 6 January, 1999.

Gooderham, Mary. "Complicated Family Ties Make Updated Will a Must." *The Globe and Mail*, 23 February, 1999: R7.

Gooderham, Mary. "Wipe Slate Clean to Put Financial House in Order." *The Globe and Mail*, 23 February, 1999: R1.

Hill, Alma E. "That Bundle of Joy Will Cost You a Bundle." *The Atlanta Constitution*, 24 March, 1998: D01.

Hope, Marty. "Young People Buying Fewer Homes." *The Examiner*, 7 November, 1998.

Hunker, Paula Gray. "Back-To-School Bargains Are All Around." *The Washington Times*, 25 August, 1998: E3.

Hunker, Paula Gray. "Resolution of Frugality; Out with Old Debts, in with New Thriftiness." *The Washington Times*, 29 December, 1998: E1.

Jackman, Philip. "The Dark Side of Credit Cards." *The Globe and Mail*, 29 December, 1998: A18.

Jackson, Kristin. "With a Little Planning, Family Vacations Can Really Feel Like Vacations." *St. Louis Post-Dispatch*, 17 May, 1998: T1.

Kahn Shelton, Sandi. "Girls and Money." *Working Mother,* September 1998: 75

Kapica, Jack. "Money Programs Much Improved." *The Globe and Mail,* 30 January, 1999: C19.

Kerr, Ann. "The Shock of Raising Baby." *The Globe and Mail,* 23 February, 1999: R1.

Landry, Jared, and Jennifer Welsh. "Young Adults Carry Protection—in RRSPs." *The Globe and Mail,* 14 January, 1999: B6.

Loggins, Kirk. "Some Tips to Help Children Learn the Value of Money." Gannett News Service, 19 January, 1996.

Maley, Dianne. "Mortgage Lenders Learning to Bend." *The Globe and Mail,* 9 April, 1996: C1.

Marron, Kevin. "It Figures: The Web's Got a New Tool for Surfers." *The Globe and Mail,* 23 February, 1999: R10.

Marron, Kevin. "Forget the Piggy Bank: Kids Want Plastic." *The Globe and Mail,* 2 December, 1998: C1.

Martin, Tony. "How to Steer Clear of Costly Blunders." *The Globe and Mail,* 9 April, 1996: C4.

Martin, Tony. "Credit Card Curb Key to Dealing with Debt." *The Globe and Mail,* 9 April, 1996: C3

McCarthy, Shawn. "Higher Bank Fees In Branches Affect Poor: Study." *The Globe and Mail,* 16 February, 1999: A2.

Miller, David. "Drowning in a Sea of Debt." *The London Free Press,* 30 March, 1998: E8-9.

Mulroney, Catherine. "When Kids Return to the Nest." *The Globe and Mail,* 2 December, 1998

"Night Owls Wealthier Than Early Birds: Study." *The Toronto Star,* 17 April, 1999: L10.

Phillips, Carol. "When Investing Is Child's Play." *The Globe and Mail,* 9 April, 1996: C1.

Pittaway, Kim, Terri Foxman, and Nathalie Robertson. "Save $5,000 in '98! (Tips From Canadian Shoppers)." *Chatelaine* 71 (January 1998): 22(7).

Ramsay, Laura. "Crafting a Long-Term Plan for Disabled Kids." *The Globe and Mail,* 2 December, 1998: C3.

Ramsay, Laura. "Growing Numbers Bear Elder Care Burden." *The Globe and Mail,* 2 December, 1998: C1.

Ray, Randy. "Easy Credit Buries Rising Number Of Young In Debt." *The Globe and Mail,* 2 December, 1998: C4.

Read, Deborah. "A Woman's Lifetime Guide to Financial Security." *Chatelaine* 67 (March 1994): 47

"Recreational Spending On Rise Despite Falling Incomes: Study." *The Examiner,* 12 February, 1999: A5.

Richards, Clay F. "Handling Money Matters. Owning/Owing: Getting Started on Firm Footing." *Newsday,* 14 March, 1999: H17.

Richter, Marice. "Married...with paychecks: New Research Reveals the (Surprisingly) Happy State of Two-Income Families." *The Dallas Morning News,* 29 August, 1996: 1C.

Rowland, Mary. "Education: Teaching Your Kids About Money." *Money,* 1 March, 1990: 126.

Satran, Pamela Redmond. "The Cheapest Women in America." *Good Housekeeping* 223: 80(4).

Schoolman, Judith. "Nag Factor Plays Major Role In Purchases For Kids." Reuters 17 August, 1998.

Silverstein, Alan. "Be Cautious— Even if It's All in the Family." *The Toronto Star,* 4 July, 1998.

Simpson, Linda, Sara Douglas, and Julie Schimmel. "Tween Consumes: Catalog Clothing Purchase Behavior." *Adolescence:* 22 September, 1998: 637(8).

Veigle, Anne. "Spending Time to Fix Spending Habits." *The Washington Times,* 25 August, 1998: E4.

Vieira, Paul. "There's Help in Untangling the Tax Web." *The Globe and Mail,* 9 April, 1996: C2.

Walton, Dawn. "Sugar and Chocolate Confectionery Industry." *The Globe and Mail,* 13 January, 1999: B6.

Welch, Stewart H. III. "Budgeting: Getting The Most From Your Earnings." *The 10 Minute Guide To Personal Finance For Newlyweds.* 1 January, 1996.

"Why an Estate Plan Is Essential to Your Family's Well-Being." *Canada Trust Investor News:* April, 1999: 3.

Yaccato, Joanne Thomas. "Here's Looking at You, Kid. *Chatelaine* 69 (June 1996): 38(1).

Yaccato, Joanne Thomas. "Take Some Credit—Maintaining Good Credit Rating." *Chatelaine* 68 (1995): 26.

Index